P9-CQX-175

The Umberto Menghi Seafood Cookbook

by Umberto Menghi
with Ron Lammie

KEY PORTER BOOKS

A DAVID ROBINSON / KEY PORTER BOOK

Copyright © 1987 by Umberto Menghi with Ron Lammie

All rights reserved. No part of this work covered by the copyrights hereon may be reproduced in any form or by any means — graphic, electronic or mechanical, including photocopying, recording, taping or information storage and retrieval systems — without the prior written permission of the publisher.

Canadian Cataloguing in Publication Data

Menghi, Umberto, 1946-
  The Umberto Menghi seafood cookbook

Includes index.
ISBN 1-55013-039-0

1. Cookery (Seafood). 2. Cookery, Italian.
I. Title. II. Title: Seafood cookbook.

TX747.M46 1987   641.6'92   C87-094212-3

Key Porter Books Limited
70 The Esplanade
Toronto, Ontario
Canada M5E 1R2

A David Robinson Book

First Printing: September 1987

Edited and designed by David Robinson
Cover and food photography by Derik Murray
Food preparation by Ron Lammie; food styling by Umberto Menghi
Typeset by Pièce de Résistance
Printed by D.W. Friesen & Sons
Printed and bound in Canada

87 88 89 90 6 5 4 3 2 1

Contents

Introduction

As a chef and restaurateur, I have always been excited by seafood. I have found it a challenge and a pleasant surprise. Seafood is one of my favourite foods. It has always been on the menu of my restaurants and, since the mid 1970s, I have had a restaurant that specializes only in seafood. In fact, it is because of the demands of my patrons that I have written this book.

Over the years, I have watched the consumption of seafood increase and for good reason. Seafood is an extremely versatile food, encompassing freshwater fish, shellfish and saltwater fish. It is a food that is readily available, no matter where you live, and available in great variety. It is adaptable to almost any cooking method — you can bake it, sauté it, pan-fry it, poach it, steam it, grill it or have it marinated cold. You can serve it as a main course, use it as an appetizer or put it in soups and salads. It is recognized as a healthy food, high in protein and low in fat content. It is a food for today's lifestyle. It is simple to prepare, takes very little cooking time and is easy to digest.

Seafood is no longer a food that is primarily known in restaurants, although restaurants are still the best way to initially experience seafood. If you try seafood in a restaurant and like what you eat, search it out in the marketplace or ask for it. If it is available to restaurants, it is available to you. Seafood is available all year round. It is not a food only to be thought of in the summertime, when it is hot and you want something light. Several varieties of seafood, particularly shellfish, are, in fact, better in the wintertime.

The most important thing to remember when buying seafood is: do not choose a fish or shellfish by its look or by its name, but, rather, by its taste. For best results in cooking, always buy seafood that is in season and that is fresh. Do not be afraid to use seafood that comes from a great distance or another part of the world. Because of advances in refrigeration and transportation, seafood can be available fresh almost anywhere in the world. Pay attention to when seafood becomes available fresh in your local market and buy it then.

Buying seafood is the most important step in your recipe. If you buy good seafood that is fresh, you will get good results with it. When buying seafood, it should always smell fresh and not have a strong odour. For whole fish, the eyes should be bright and shiny; the skin and gills, vibrant, not dull. The fish should be firm to the touch, not soft. Shellfish should be cooked live — or as next to live as possible. Fillets of fish should be firm, elastic. There should be no trace of oil on their surface. Whole fish and fillets should be kept in plastic and refrigerated. This will keep them moist and keep their odour to themselves. Seafood should be used as it is bought — it should not be kept. It may be frozen, however. If you freeze fish, thaw it at room temperature. When cooking with whole fish, save the bones and make fish stock.

Never overcook seafood. The three best things about seafood are: its tenderness; its moistness; its sweetness. Always, you want to cook to maintain those things. All cooking times in this book are approximate, depending on the size of the fish; the thickness of the fillet; the amount of heat in cooking. The recipes in this book use very little oil or liquid, fast reductions, fresh herbs, and light, not thick, sauces — sauces that complement or accentuate the seafood, not over-power it.

We hope you enjoy this book. We have tried to create it with a certain amount of flair and invite you, in using it, to be adventurous with seafood. You will not be disappointed!

Umberto Menghi
Vancouver, B.C.
July, 1987

Stocks & Sauces

CHICKEN STOCK
Consommé di Pollo

Makes 8 cups/2 L

2 lbs./1 kg chicken bones	*Rinse chicken bones under cold running water and put in a pot.*
1 small onion, peeled and chopped 1 small carrot, peeled and chopped 1 stalk of celery, washed and chopped	*Add onion, carrot and celery to pot.*
12 cups/3 L cold water	*Add water to pot and bring to a boil. Skim foam from top of pot.*
1/2 tsp./2 mL salt 1/2 tsp./2 mL cracked white peppercorns 1 bay leaf 1 sprig of fresh thyme, chopped	*Season with salt, peppercorns, bay leaf and thyme.*
	Reduce heat and simmer over low heat for 1-2 hours, then strain contents of pot through a sieve lined with a linen or muslin cloth into a plastic container.

Chicken stock is used in many of the recipes in this book. Make it ahead and always have it on hand. Chicken stock may be stored in a sealed plastic container in the refrigerator for approximately 1 week.

FISH STOCK
Consommé di Pesce

Makes 8 cups/2 L

3-4 lbs./1.5-2 kg fish bones — no skin	*Rinse fish bones under cold running water for 5-10 minutes, then set aside.*
1/2 tbsp./7 mL cracked white peppercorns 1 bay leaf 3 whole stalks of fresh parsley	*Put peppercorns, bay leaf and parsley in the bottom of a pot.*
1 medium onion, peeled and chopped 1 medium carrot, peeled and chopped	*Cover with onion and carrot.*
	Cover with fish bones.
3/4 cup/175 mL dry white wine	*Add white wine to pot and bring to a boil. Reduce heat and simmer for 5-10 minutes.*
8 cups/2 L cold water	*Add water to pot and bring to a boil. Reduce heat and simmer for 20-25 minutes, then strain contents of pot through a sieve lined with a linen or muslin cloth into a plastic container.*

Fish stock is used in several of the recipes in this book. Make it ahead and always have it on hand. Fish stock may be stored in a sealed plastic container in the refrigerator for approximately 1 week.

BECHAMEL SAUCE
Salsa Bianca

Makes 2 cups/500 mL

4 tbsp./60 mL butter	*Melt butter in a saucepan and remove saucepan from heat.*
4 tbsp./60 mL flour	*Add flour, sprinkling at first, to saucepan and, using a whisk, blend in to form a roux.*
2 cups/500 mL warm milk	*Add warm milk, a little at a time, to saucepan and blend in.*
	Return saucepan to heat and simmer, whisking frequently, until sauce is thick and smooth.

salt *(to taste)*	*Season with salt, pepper and nutmeg.*
white pepper *(to taste)*	
1/8 tsp./pinch of ground nutmeg	
dash of Worcestershire sauce	*Add Worcestershire sauce to saucepan and blend in.*
	Strain contents of saucepan through a sieve into another saucepan and set aside.

Béchamel sauce is used in several of the recipes in this book. Always make it fresh when it is called for. The portions are: equal parts butter and flour to milk. The ratio is approximately four to one: four parts milk to one part butter and flour. Make Béchamel sauce ahead of time in any recipe that calls for it and warm when needed.

SAUCE VERTE
Salsa Verde

Makes 2 cups/500 mL

6-8 leaves of fresh spinach, washed and stemmed	*Blanch leaves of spinach in a pot of rapidly boiling water for 10 seconds, then drain pot and squeeze spinach dry.*
	Put spinach in a blender.
5 sprigs of watercress, washed and dried	*Add watercress to blender.*
1 tbsp./15 mL finely chopped fresh parsley	*Add parsley, chervil and tarragon to blender and purée, then transfer contents of blender to a bowl.*
1 tbsp./15 mL finely chopped fresh chervil	
1 tbsp./15 mL finely chopped fresh tarragon	
1 1/2 cups/375 mL mayonnaise (see p. 14)	*Add mayonnaise to bowl and blend in.*
1 tsp./5 mL freshly squeezed lemon juice	*Add lemon juice, Worcestershire sauce and Tabasco sauce to bowl and blend in.*
2 drops of Worcestershire sauce	
1 drop of Tabasco sauce	
salt *(to taste)*	*Season with salt and pepper.*
white pepper *(to taste)*	
	Cover bowl with plastic wrap and store in the refrigerator until ready to use.

TARTAR SAUCE
Salsa Tartara

Makes 2 cups/500 mL

1 1/4 cups/300 mL mayonnaise *(see p. 14)*	*Put mayonnaise in a bowl.*
1 hardboiled egg, finely grated 1 fillet of anchovy, washed and finely chopped 1 medium dill pickle, finely chopped 1 tbsp./15 mL drained capers 1 tbsp./15 mL finely chopped fresh parsley 1 tbsp./15 mL chopped fresh chives 1 tbsp./15 mL fresh lemon thyme	*Add grated egg, anchovies, pickle, capers, parsley, chives and lemon thyme to bowl and mix together thoroughly.*
salt *(to taste)* white pepper *(to taste)*	*Season with salt and pepper.*
	Cover bowl with plastic wrap and put in the refrigerator for at least 2 hours before serving.
2 tbsp./30 mL whipping cream *(optional)*	*If sauce is too thick, thin by adding cream to bowl and blending in.*

TOMATO SAUCE
Salsa di Pomodoro

Makes 4 cups/1 L

1 large onion,
peeled and finely chopped
1 tbsp./15 mL olive oil
1 tbsp./15 mL butter

Sauté onion in oil and butter in a saucepan for 2-3 minutes until soft and transparent.

1 medium carrot,
peeled and finely chopped
1 stalk of celery,
washed, threaded and finely chopped

Add carrot and celery to saucepan and sauté for approximately 5 minutes.

1 (28 oz./796 mL) can of peeled
and finely chopped peeled Italian
plum tomatoes — and tomato liquid
2 tbsp./30 mL tomato paste
2 cloves of garlic, peeled and minced
1 bay leaf
1/2 tsp./2 mL finely chopped
fresh basil
1 tsp./5 mL finely chopped
fresh oregano
1 whole clove, crushed
1 tbsp./15 mL sugar
1/2 cup/125 mL dry red wine

Add tomatoes, tomato liquid, tomato paste, garlic, bay leaf, basil, oregano, clove, sugar and red wine to saucepan and bring to a boil. Reduce heat and simmer, uncovered, for approximately 1 hour.

salt *(to taste)*
freshly ground black pepper *(to taste)*

Season with salt and pepper.

Strain sauce through a fine sieve into a plastic container. Sauce should be thick and rich. If sauce is too thin after straining, return to saucepan and continue to simmer until sauce reaches the desired consistency. If sauce is too thick, thin by adding a little water.

1 tbsp./15 mL olive oil

Top container with olive oil, but do not blend in. Allow sauce to cool, uncovered and unrefrigerated, for 4 hours, then seal and store in the refrigerator until ready to use.

Tomato sauce is used in many of the recipes in this book. Make it ahead and always have it on hand. Tomato sauce may be stored in a sealed plastic container in the refrigerator for approximately 1 week.

WHITE WINE SAUCE   *Makes 2 cups/500 mL*
Salsa al Vino Bianco

1 tbsp./15 mL peeled and finely chopped shallots 1/2 tsp./2 mL finely chopped fresh tarragon 8 whole marinated green peppercorns, mashed 1 1/2 cups/375 mL dry white wine	*Simmer shallots, tarragon and peppercorns in white wine until wine has reduced by one-half. Set aside.*
1 1/2 tbsp./20 mL butter	*Melt butter in a saucepan and remove saucepan from heat.*
2 tbsp./30 mL flour	*Add flour, sprinkling at first, to saucepan and, using a whisk, blend in to form a roux.*
3/4 cup/175 mL fish stock *(see p. 8)*	*Add fish stock, a little at a time, to saucepan and blend in.*
	Return saucepan to heat. Add wine mixture to saucepan and simmer, whisking frequently, until sauce is thick and smooth.
1/2 cup/125 mL whipping cream	*Add cream to saucepan and blend in. Simmer for 2-3 minutes.*
salt *(to taste)* white pepper *(to taste)*	*Season with salt and pepper.*
	Strain sauce through a sieve into a plastic container.
1/4 tsp./1 mL butter	*Put a small amount of butter on top of sauce in container to prevent a skim from forming.*
	Seal and store in the refrigerator until ready to use.

White wine sauce is used in several of the recipes in this book. Make it ahead and have it on hand. White wine sauce may be stored in a sealed plastic container in the refrigerator for approximately 1 week.

GARLIC MAYONNAISE
Salsa Aioli

Makes 2 cups/500 mL

2 egg yolks — at room temperature	*Break egg yolks with a fork in a bowl.*
1 1/2 tbsp./20 mL peeled and finely chopped garlic 1/2 tsp./2 mL salt 1/8 tsp./pinch of white pepper	*Add garlic, salt and pepper to bowl and mix together.*
1 1/2 cups/375 mL olive oil	*Add oil, drop by drop at first, to bowl and, using a whisk, blend in. Add more oil only when previous oil has blended in. After the first spoonfuls of oil have been blended in, mayonnaise should become quite thick. Oil can be added more freely now — in a steady stream, whisking constantly, until all the oil is used.*
1 tsp./5 mL freshly squeezed lemon juice 2 tbsp./30 mL dry white wine	*Add lemon juice and white wine to bowl and blend in.*
2 tbsp./30 mL cold water *(optional)*	*If mayonnaise is too thick, thin by adding water to bowl and blending in.*
salt *(to taste)* white pepper *(to taste)*	*Taste and adjust seasoning with salt and pepper.*
	Cover bowl with plastic wrap and store in the refrigerator until ready to use.

HERBED MAYONNAISE
Maionese con Erbe Fini

Makes 2 cups/500 mL

1 1/2 cups/375 mL mayonnaise *(see below)*	*Put mayonnaise in a bowl.*
1/2 tsp./2 mL finely chopped fresh parsley 1 tbsp./15 mL chopped fresh chives 1 tsp./5 mL finely chopped fresh chervil 1 tsp./4 mL finely chopped fresh dill 1 /2 tsp./2 mL finely chopped fresh tarragon 1/4 tsp./1 mL fresh thyme	*Add parsley, chives, chervil, dill, tarragon and thyme to bowl and mix together thoroughly.*
	Cover bowl with plastic wrap and store in the refrigerator until ready to use.

MAYONNAISE
Maionese

Makes 2 cups/500 mL

2 egg yolks — at room temperature	*Break egg yolks with a fork in a bowl.*
1 tbsp./15 mL Dijon mustard 1/4 tsp./1 mL salt 1/8 tsp./pinch of white pepper	*Add mustard, salt and pepper to bowl and blend in.*
1 1/2 cups/375 mL light oil	*Add oil, drop by drop at first, to bowl and, using a whisk, blend in. Add more oil only when previous oil has blended in. After the first spoonfuls of oil have been blended in, mayonnaise should become quite thick. Oil can be added more freely now — in a steady stream, whisking constantly, until all the oil is used.*
1 tsp./5 mL freshly squeezed lemon juice 2 tsp./10 mL white wine vinegar	*Add lemon juice and wine vinegar to bowl and blend in.*
salt *(to taste)* white pepper *(to taste)*	*Taste and adjust seasoning with salt and pepper.*
	Cover bowl with plastic wrap and store in the refrigerator until ready to use.

Appetizers

COD SEVICHE WITH LIME JUICE, OLIVES AND FRESH HERBS
Serves 8
Merluzzo Marinato con Succo di Cedro, Olive e Erbe Fini

1 lb./500 g fillet of fresh cod, bones removed — cut into 1/2 inch/1 cm cubes	*Rinse cubes of cod under cold running water and pat dry with paper towels. Put in a bowl.*
4 tbsp./60 mL extra virgin olive oil	*Add olive oil to bowl and, using a wooden spoon, gently mix to coat cod with oil.*
1 tbsp./15 mL finely chopped fresh parsley 1 tbsp./15 mL finely chopped fresh basil 1 tbsp./15 mL finely chopped fresh cilantro	*Add parsley, basil and cilantro to bowl and mix together.*
1/2-1 Jalapeño green pepper, seeded and finely chopped	*Add green pepper to bowl and mix together.*
10 black Calamata olives, pitted and sliced 6 green Calamata olives, pitted and sliced	*Add black and green olives to bowl and mix together.*
salt *(to taste)* freshly ground black pepper *(to taste)*	*Season with salt and pepper.*
juice of 4 limes	*Add lime juice to bowl and gently mix together.*
	Put bowl in the refrigerator and allow cod to marinate in lime juice for 24 hours. Stir occasionally.
8 thinly sliced onion rings 1 small red pepper, seeded and sliced into rings 1 small green pepper seeded and sliced into rings 2 limes, cut into 8 wedges juice of 1 lime	*Remove bowl from refrigerator and, using a slotted spoon, transfer contents of bowl to a platter. Garnish platter with onion rings, rings of red and green pepper and lime wedges. Freshen cod by sprinkling with lime juice and serve immediately. Serve directly from platter to individual plates.*

FISH PATE
Budino di Pesce

Serves 8

1 lb./500 g fillet of any fresh white fish, skin and bones removed — cod, halibut, red snapper or sole	*Rinse fillet under cold running water and pat dry with paper towels. Put in a blender or food processor and process until a fine paste is formed.*
2 egg whites	*Add egg whites to blender or food processor and blend in.*
2 cups/500 mL whipping cream	*Add cream to blender or food processor and blend in, then transfer contents of blender or food processor to a bowl.*
juice of 1 lemon dash of Worcestershire sauce	*Add lemon juice and Worcestershire sauce to bowl and blend by hand.*
salt *(to taste)* white pepper *(to taste)* 1/8 tsp./pinch of mace	*Season with salt, pepper and mace. Set bowl aside.*
2 bunches of fresh spinach, washed and stemmed 1/4 cup/50 mL dry white wine juice of 1/2 lemon	*Cook spinach in a pot containing white wine and lemon juice for approximately 1 minute until spinach has just wilted, then drain pot and put spinach in the blender or food processor.*
	Add one-half of the fish mixture to spinach in blender or food processor and process until smooth.
	Pre-heat oven to 350°F/180°C.
buttered paper	*Put spinach-fish mixture in the bottom of a rectangular shaped buttered mold. Put remaining fish mixture on top of spinach-fish mixture. Put mold in a pan of hot water that comes halfway up the sides of the mold. Cover mold with a sheet of buttered paper.*
	Put pan containing mold in the oven and bake for approximately 25 minutes until pâté is firm. Remove pan from oven. Remove mold from water. Allow mold to cool, then turn out pâté on a cutting board.
2 cups/500 mL coulis of tomatoes *(see next page)*	*Put 1/4 cup/50 mL coulis of tomatoes on 8 individual plates.*

Cut pâté into 1 inch/2 cm thick slices and put on top of coulis of tomatoes on plates. Serve immediately.

Coulis of Tomatoes:

8 firm, ripe tomatoes, eyes removed, and scored "x" on top	*Blanch tomatoes in a pot of rapidly boiling water for 20 seconds, then plunge into a pot of cold water to stop the cooking. Peel and seed tomatoes, then put them in a blender or food processor and purée.*
3 tbsp./45 mL extra virgin olive oil 1 tbsp./15 mL white wine vinegar	*Add oil and vinegar to blender and mix together.*
1 tbsp./15 mL finely chopped fresh parsley	*Add parsley to blender and mix together.*
salt *(to taste)* freshly ground black pepper *(to taste)*	*Season with salt and pepper.*

MUSSELS, PRAWNS, SCALLOPS, SQUID AND HOT RED CHILI PEPPERS MARINATED IN WHITE WINE, LEMON JUICE, GARLIC AND FRESH HERBS
Serves 8
Frutti di Mare

3/4-1 lb./350-500 g fresh squid — 8 squid	*Clean squid by pulling off the head and pulling out the entrails. Discard head and entrails. Remove quill from squid and discard. Lay squid on a cutting board or flat surface and, using a sharp knife, scrape the membrane off. Rinse squid thoroughly under cold running water. Cut off tentacles in front of eyes and reserve. Make sure beak-like mouth is discarded. Chop tentacles, if large. Chop body into 1/2 inch/1 cm rounds. Pat squid dry with a cloth or paper towel. Set aside.*
1/2 onion, peeled and thinly sliced — separated into rings 1 tbsp./15 mL olive oil	*Sauté onion in oil in a pot for 2-3 minutes until soft and transparent.*

(cont'd over)

1/2 lb./250 g fresh mussels,
washed and cleaned — 16 mussels
1 lb./500 g fresh jumbo prawn tails,
shells left on
— 16 prawn tails
1/2 lb./250 g large fresh scallops
— 16 scallops

Add squid to pot and sauté for 3-4 minutes, then add mussels, prawns and scallops to pot, cover and steam for 5-6 minutes until mussels open. Discard any mussels that do not open.

1 cup/250 mL dry white wine
juice of 2 lemons
1 tsp./5 mL peeled and
finely chopped garlic
2 tbsp./30 mL finely chopped
fresh parsley
salt *(to taste)*
freshly ground black pepper *(to taste)*

Add white wine, lemon juice, garlic, parsley, salt and pepper to pot and simmer, uncovered, for approximately 2 minutes, then transfer contents of pot to a bowl.

1/2-1 tsp./2-5 mL seeded and finely
chopped hot red chili pepper
1 tbsp./15 mL washed and
chopped scallions
1 tbsp./15 mL finely chopped fresh dill

Add chili pepper, scallions and dill to bowl and gently mix together.

Put bowl in the refrigerator and allow seafood to marinate in wine for 4 hours.

Remove bowl from refrigerator and, using a slotted spoon, transfer contents of bowl to a platter.

1 large firm, ripe tomato,
eye removed and scored "x" on top

Before serving, blanch tomato in a pot of rapidly boiling water for 20 seconds, then plunge into a pot of cold water to stop the cooking. Peel, seed and julienne tomato.

Garnish seafood on platter with julienned tomato and serve immediately. Serve directly from platter to individual plates.

SHRIMP AND ZUCCHINI TART
Crostata di Gamberetti e Zucchini

Serves 8

Pie Crust:

2 cups/500 mL flour
1/2 tsp./2 mL salt
1/4 tsp./1 mL baking powder
2 tbsp./30 mL sugar

Mix flour, salt, baking powder and sugar together in a bowl.

3/4 cup/175 mL butter

Using a pastry blender, cut butter into bowl and mix together until crumbly.

9 tbsp./135 mL ice-cold water

Add water, a little at a time, to bowl, using just enough water to bind mixture, until a dough is formed. Roll dough into a ball and handle as little as possible. Using a rolling pin, roll out dough to 1/4 inch/6 mm even thickness.

butter *(to coat)*
flour *(to dust)*

Butter the bottom of a 9 inch/23 cm pie plate and lightly dust with flour.

Pre-heat oven to 350°F/180°C.

Put dough in pie plate and, using fingertips, gently press into the shape of the plate. Prick dough with a fork in several places. Put pie plate in oven and pre-bake pie shell for approximately 8 minutes until lightly golden. Remove pie plate from oven and set aside.

Filling:

1 medium zucchini,
washed and julienned
1/2 lb./250 g fresh shrimp

Fill bottom of pie shell with zucchini and shrimp.

salt *(to taste)*
freshly ground black pepper *(to taste)*
1/4 tsp./1 mL fresh thyme

Season with salt, pepper and thyme. Set pie shell aside.

2 large eggs
1 cup/250 mL whipping cream

Beat eggs and cream together in a bowl.

1/8 tsp./pinch of ground nutmeg

Season with nutmeg.

Pour egg mixture over zucchini and shrimp in pie shell and set aside.

(cont'd over)

1/4 cup/50 mL freshly grated
Fontina cheese
1/4 cup/50 mL freshly grated
Gruyère cheese
1/4 cup/50 mL freshly grated
Mozzarella cheese

Mix Fontina, Gruyère and Mozzarella cheeses together in a bowl.

Sprinkle cheese over egg mixture.

crisp green salad *(to accompany)*

Put pie plate in oven and bake for 20-25 minutes until pie is firm. Remove from oven and allow pie to sit for approximately 10 minutes before serving. Cut into wedges and serve on 8 individual plates. Serve with a crisp green salad on the side.

SHRIMP CANAPES
Crostini di Gamberetti

Makes 16

1 lb./500 g fresh shrimp
— reserving 16 whole shrimp
for garnish
2 egg yolks
juice of 2 lemons
1/4 cup/50 mL brandy
2 tbsp./30 mL finely chopped
fresh parsley
4 dashes of Tabasco sauce

Put shrimp, egg yolks, lemon juice, brandy, parsley and Tabasco sauce in a blender or food processor and process until a fine paste is formed.

salt *(to taste)*
freshly ground black pepper *(to taste)*

Season with salt and pepper and set aside.

Pre-heat oven to broil/grill.

1 baguette of French bread
— cut into 16 thin slices

Put slices of bread on a baking sheet and toast in oven until golden.

Remove baking sheet from oven and allow bread to cool slightly, then spread shrimp mixture on top of each slice of bread to make canapés.

16 black olive rings
16 whole shrimp *(reserved above)*
2 lemons, cut into 8 wedges

Put canapés on a platter. Garnish each canapé with 1 black olive ring and 1 whole shrimp. Garnish platter with lemon wedges and serve immediately.

SEAFOOD COCKTAIL
Cocktail di Mare Casino

Serves 8

1 lb./500 g fresh shrimp 1 lb./500 g fresh crabmeat	*Put shrimp and crabmeat in a bowl and gently mix together.*
1 head of butter or Boston lettuce, washed and dried — 8 whole leaves	*Put 1 whole leaf of lettuce in the bottom of 8 individual glass serving dishes.*
	Put seafood mixture on top of lettuce in each dish.
casino sauce *(see below)*	*Spoon sauce over seafood mixture to cover.*
2 lemons, cut into 8 wedges	*Garnish the rim of each dish with 1 lemon wedge and serve immediately.*

Casino Sauce:

2 hardboiled egg yolks	*Mash egg yolks with a fork in a bowl.*
2 tsp./10 mL Dijon mustard	*Add mustard to bowl and blend in.*
6 tbsp./90 mL vegetable oil	*Add oil, drop by drop at first, to bowl and blend in.*
juice of 2 lemons	*Add lemon juice to bowl and blend in.*
6 tbsp./90 mL ketchup 2 tbsp./30 mL whipping cream 2 tbsp./30 mL dry sherry 3 dashes of Worcestershire sauce	*Add ketchup, cream, sherry and Worcestershire sauce to bowl and blend in.*
salt *(to taste)* freshly ground black pepper *(to taste)* 1/8 tsp./pinch of paprika	*Season with salt, pepper and paprika.*
	Cover bowl with plastic wrap and chill in the refrigerator until ready to use.

SMOKED SALMON STUFFED
WITH RICOTTA CHEESE AND CHIVES   *Serves 8*
Salmone Affumicato con Ricotta

1 lb./500 g sliced fresh smoked salmon
— 16 slices large enough to stuff

Lay each slice of smoked salmon on a large sheet of waxed paper and set aside.

1 lb./500 g fresh Ricotta cheese
juice of 1/2 orange
1 tbsp./15 mL Dijon mustard
1/2 cup/125 mL chopped fresh chives

Mix Ricotta cheese, orange juice, mustard and chives together in a bowl.

salt *(to taste)*
white pepper *(to taste)*

Season with salt and pepper.

Spoon Ricotta cheese mixture on top of each slice of smoked salmon to fill the slice crosswise, then roll each slice.

1 head of butter or Boston lettuce, washed and dried — 8 whole leaves

Put 1 whole leaf of lettuce in middle of 8 individual plates.

Lay 2 rolls of smoked salmon, side by side, seam side down, across each leaf of lettuce.

32 thinly sliced red onion rings
5 tbsp./75 mL drained capers

Garnish each roll of smoked salmon with 2 red onion rings and 1 tsp./5 mL capers.

5 tbsp./75 mL extra virgin olive oil

Drizzle rolls with olive oil.

2 lemons, cut into 16 thin wedges

Garnish each plate with 2 lemon wedges — 1 wedge per roll — and serve immediately.

STURGEON GRAVLAX
MARINATED WITH BRANDY AND DILL   *Serves 8*
Fette di Storione Marinato con Salsa Norvegese

2 (1 lb./500 g) fillets of fresh sturgeon	*Rinse fillets of sturgeon under cold running water and pat dry with paper towels. Set aside.*
1 1/2 tbsp./20 mL coarse salt 1 tsp./5 mL cracked white peppercorns 2 1/2 tbsp./40 mL sugar	*Mix salt, peppercorns and sugar together in a bowl. Rub seasoning mixture into sturgeon.*
1 tbsp./15 mL brandy 1 tbsp./15 mL vegetable oil	*Rub fillets with brandy and vegetable oil.*
1 bunch of fresh dill	*Put 1 fillet in a baking dish. Lay dill on top of this fillet. Cover fillet with other fillet. Put a wooden board on top of both fillets and put a 5-10 lb./2.5-5 kg weight on top of board.*
	Put baking dish in the refrigerator and allow sturgeon to marinate in brandy and dill for 48 hours. Turn fillets over approximately every 6 hours.
	Remove baking dish from refrigerator. Remove wooden board and weight from sturgeon and put sturgeon on a cutting board.
sprigs of fresh dill 2 lemons, cut into 8 wedges	*Cut sturgeon into thin slices and arrange on a platter. Garnish each slice of sturgeon with 1 sprig of dill. Garnish platter with lemon wedges and serve immediately.*

Leftover gravlax may be frozen and served at some other time.

TOMATOES STUFFED WITH SEAFOOD
SERVED WITH FRESH MINT
Pomodori Ripieni di Pesce alla Menta

Serves 8

8 large firm, ripe tomatoes, eyes removed and scored "x" on top

Blanch tomatoes in a pot of rapidly boiling water for 20 seconds, then plunge into a pot of cold water to stop the cooking. Peel and cut the tops off tomatoes, 1/2 inch/1 cm from top. Remove pulp from tomatoes and discard. Set tomato shells aside.

1/2 lb./250 g fresh shrimp
1/2 lb./250 g fresh crabmeat
1 stalk of celery, washed, threaded and finely chopped
1/2 cup/125 mL fresh or canned petits pois
1 lemon, peeled, seeded and cut in chunks
4 tbsp./60 mL mayonnaise *(see p. 14)*

Put shrimp, crabmeat, celery, petits pois, chunks of lemon and mayonnaise in a bowl and gently mix together.

salt *(to taste)*
freshly ground black pepper *(to taste)*
1 tsp./5 mL paprika

Season with salt, pepper and paprika.

Spoon seafood mixture into tomato shells.

8 small fresh mint leaves

Garnish each shell with 1 mint leaf.

2 cups/500 mL coulis of tomatoes *(see p. 17)*

Put 1/4 cup/50 mL coulis of tomatoes on 8 individual plates.

2 lemons, cut into 8 wedges

Put stuffed tomatoes on top of coulis of tomatoes on plates. Garnish plates with lemon wedges and serve immediately.

TUNA AND CHEESE CANAPES
Crostini di Tonno con Formaggio

Makes 16

1/2-3/4 lb./250-350 g thinly sliced fillet of fresh tuna — 16 slices

Cut slices of tuna into the shape of baguette and set aside.

6 tbsp./90 mL butter

*Melt butter in a saucepan.
Do not burn.*

2 tbsp./30 mL drained horseradish

Add horseradish to butter and blend in. Set saucepan aside and keep warm.

Pre-heat oven to broil/grill.

1 baguette of French bread — cut into 16 slices	*Put slices of bread on a baking sheet and toast slightly in oven.*
	Remove baking sheet from oven and brush bread with horseradish butter.
2 tbsp./30 mL dry red wine	*Drizzle bread with red wine.*
	Put slices of tuna on top of bread.
3-4 balls of fresh Mozzarella cheese, cut into 16 thin slices — the shape of the baguette	*Put slices of cheese on top of tuna to make canapés.*
	Return baking sheet to oven and broil/grill until cheese melts.
freshly ground black pepper *(to taste)*	*Remove baking sheet from oven and put canapés on a platter. Grind fresh pepper over top of cheese and serve immediately.*

TUNA CARPACCIO
WITH AVOCADO AND MUSTARD SAUCE *Serves 8*
Carpaccio di Tonno con Senape

1 lb./500 g very thinly sliced fillet of fresh tuna—32 slices of tuna carpaccio	*Arrange slices of tuna on a platter, overlapping the slices, and set aside.*
2 small avocados, peeled and pitted	*Mash avocados with a fork in a bowl.*
4 tbsp./60 mL extra virgin olive oil juice of 2 lemons 2 tbsp./30 mL dry white wine 3 tbsp./45 mL Dijon mustard	*Add olive oil, lemon juice, white wine and mustard to bowl and mix together until well blended.*
1/4-1/2 cup/50-125 mL chicken stock *(see p. 7)*	*Add chicken stock to bowl and blend in until sauce has a medium consistency, neither thick nor thin.*
salt *(to taste)* white pepper *(to taste)*	*Season with salt and pepper.*
	Pour sauce over tuna on platter.
6 fresh mushrooms, cleaned and sliced paper thin 12 slivers of fresh Parmesan cheese 1 tbsp./15 mL finely chopped fresh parsley 8 slices of French bread *(to accompany)*	*Sprinkle with mushrooms, slivers of Parmesan cheese and parsley and serve immediately. Serve directly from platter to individual plates. Serve with French bread.*

Soups

CREAM OF MUSSEL SOUP
Cozze alla Crema

Serves 4

4-5 lbs./2-2.5 kg fresh mussels, washed and cleaned	*Set mussels aside.*
1/2 cup/125 mL peeled and finely chopped onion 1 baby carrot, peeled and finely chopped 1 stalk of celery, washed, threaded and finely chopped 2 tbsp./30 mL butter	*Sauté onion, carrot, celery and garlic in a pot for 2-3 minutes until onion is soft and transparent.*
	Add mussels to pot.
1/2 cup/125 mL dry white wine juice of 1 lemon 1 cup/250 mL whipping cream 2 tbsp./30 mL finely chopped fresh parsley 1/4 tsp./1 mL saffron threads	*Add white wine, lemon juice, cream, parsley and saffron to pot. Cover pot and steam mussels for 5-6 minutes until their shells open. Discard any mussels that do not open.*
1 tbsp./15 mL butter	*Add butter to pot and blend in.*
salt *(to taste)* freshly ground black pepper *(to taste)*	*Season with salt and pepper.*
	Transfer contents of pot to a serving bowl and serve immediately. Serve directly from serving bowl to individual bowls.

FISH STEW IN CLEAR BROTH
Brodetto di Pesce

Serves 6

1/2 lb./250 g fresh squid — 3-4 squid

Clean squid by pulling off the head and pulling out the entrails. Discard head and entrails. Remove quill from squid and discard. Lay squid on a cutting board or flat surface and, using a sharp knife, scrape the membrane off. Rinse squid thoroughly under cold running water. Cut off tentacles in front of eyes and reserve. Make sure beak-like mouth is discarded. Chop tentacles, if large. Chop body into 1/2 inch/1 cm rounds. Pat squid dry with a cloth or paper towel. Set aside.

1/2 lb./250 g fillet of fresh cod *(tail end)*, bones removed — cut into 2 inch/5 cm pieces
1/2 lb./250 g fillet of fresh red snapper, bones removed — cut into 2 inch/5 cm pieces
1/2 lb./250 g fillet of fresh sea bass, bones removed — cut into 2 inch/ 5 cm pieces

Put cod, red snapper and sea bass in a bowl and set aside.

1/2 lb./250 g fresh shrimp

Put shrimp in a bowl and set aside.

4 firm, ripe tomatoes, eyes removed and scored "x" on top

Blanch tomatoes in a pot of rapidly boiling water for 20 seconds, then plunge into a pot of cold water to stop the cooking. Peel, seed and chop tomatoes. Set aside.

1 medium onion, peeled and finely chopped
4 cloves of garlic, peeled and finely chopped
1/4 cup/50 mL olive oil

Sauté onion and garlic in oil in a pot for 2-3 minutes until onion is soft and transparent.

Add tomatoes to pot.

2 tbsp./30 mL finely chopped fresh parsley

Add parsley to pot and stir in.

Bring contents of pot to a boil. Reduce heat and simmer for approximately 5 minutes.

(cont'd over)

salt *(to taste)* freshly ground black pepper *(to taste)*	*Season with salt and pepper.*
1 cup/250 mL dry white wine 1 cup/250 mL cold water 2 cups/500 mL fish stock *(see p. 8)*	*Add white wine, water and fish stock to pot and stir in.*
	Add squid to pot.
	Bring contents of pot to a boil. Reduce heat and simmer for approximately 15 minutes.
	Add cod, red snapper and sea bass to pot. Cover pot and simmer for approximately 5 minutes, then uncover and simmer for an additional 15 minutes.
	Add shrimp to pot and stir in.
salt *(to taste)* freshly ground black pepper *(to taste)*	*Taste and adjust seasoning with salt and pepper.*
	Using a slotted spoon, gently remove fish from broth and put in a bowl. Set aside and keep warm. Allow broth to cool a little.
fried bread *(see below)*	*Divide individual fish as equally as possible among individual soup bowls. Ladle broth on top of fish in bowls and serve immediately. Serve with fried bread on plates on the side.*
Fried Bread:	
olive oil *(to coat)*	*Coat the bottom of a skillet with olive oil.*
6 slices of stale French bread, crusts removed	*Fry bread in oil in skillet until golden, then remove from skillet and drain on paper towels. Serve warm.*

HERB AND VEGETABLE SOUP
WITH SCAMPI
Scampi in Brodetto

Serves 4

1/2 lb./250 g peeled and deveined fresh or frozen scampi, thawed, if frozen — 8 scampi

Rinse scampi under cold running water and set aside to drain.

1/2 medium onion, peeled and diced
2 cloves of garlic, peeled and crushed
2 leeks, washed and chopped — use only the white part
2 tbsp./30 mL olive oil

Sauté onion, garlic and leeks in oil in a pot for 2-3 minutes until onion and leeks are soft and transparent.

4 fillets of anchovy, washed and mashed

Add anchovies to pot and stir in.

1 cup/250 mL dry white wine

Add white wine to pot and stir in. Simmer for approximately 2 minutes.

2 cups/500 mL cold water

Add water to pot and blend in.

2 sprigs of fresh parsley
2 sprigs of fresh thyme
1 bay leaf, crushed

Season with parsley, thyme and bay leaf.

1 cup/250 mL fish stock (*see p. 8*)

Add fish stock to pot and blend in.

Bring contents of pot to a boil.

Add scampi to pot.

2 hearts of butter or Boston lettuce, washed and sliced

Add hearts of lettuce to pot.

Reduce heat and simmer contents of pot for approximately 3 minutes.

salt (*to taste*)
freshly ground black pepper (*to taste*)

Season with salt and pepper.

2 tbsp./30 mL finely chopped fresh parsley

Ladle contents of pot into individual soup bowls — 2 scampi per bowl. Sprinkle with parsley and serve immediately.

LOBSTER BISQUE
Vellutata d' Astaco

Serves 6

3 (1 lb./500 g) fresh lobsters	*Using a large kitchen knife, kill lobsters by cutting them in half lengthwise from head to tail. Remove entrails from lobster by mouth and discard. Crack claws by using the flat side of knife. Remove meat from claws and coarsely chop. Set aside. Reserve shell of claws and set aside. Remove meat from tail and coarsely chop. Set aside. Reserve shell of tail and set aside. Discard remaining carcass.*
1/4 cup/50 mL olive oil 1/2 cup/125 mL butter	*Sauté lobster shells — claws and tail — in oil and butter in an ovenproof skillet for approximately 10 minutes.*
1 medium red onion, peeled and coarsely chopped 1 medium carrot, peeled and coarsely chopped 1 stalk of celery, washed and coarsely chopped 1 small clove of garlic, peeled and coarsely chopped	*Add onion, carrot, celery and garlic to skillet and sauté for approximately 10 minutes.*
	Pre-heat oven to 300°F/150°C.
1/2 cup/125 mL butter	*Add butter to skillet.*
	Put skillet in oven and roast shells, stirring occasionally, for 1 1/2 hours. Be careful not to burn shells. Remove skillet from oven.
1/2 cup/125 mL brandy	*Add brandy to skillet and flambé.*
2 cups/500 mL dry white wine 1/2 cup/125 mL dry sherry	*When flame dies down, add white wine and sherry to skillet and deglaze skillet, then transfer contents of skillet to a pot.*
2 tbsp./30 mL tomato paste	*Add tomato paste to pot and blend in.*
3 tbsp./45 mL flour	*Sprinkle with flour and blend in.*
2 very ripe fresh tomatoes, peeled, seeded and chopped 6 cleaned whole fresh mushrooms	*Add tomatoes and mushrooms to pot and stir in.*

8 cups/2 L fish stock *(see p. 8)* or cold water	*Add fish stock or water to pot and stir in.*
2 sprigs of fresh parsley 1 sprig of fresh tarragon 1 sprig of fresh thyme 1 bay leaf white pepper *(to taste)* 1/8 tsp./pinch of cayenne	*Season with parsley, tarragon, thyme, bay leaf, white pepper and cayenne.*
	Bring contents of pot to a boil. Skim pot. Reduce heat to a slow boil and cook for approximately 1 hour. If liquid reduces too much, add water.
	Strain contents of pot through a sieve lined with a linen or muslin cloth into another pot.
1 cup/250 mL whipping cream	*Add cream to pot, blend in and heat until soup has the desired consistency. Set pot aside and keep warm.*
1 tbsp./15 mL olive oil 2 tbsp./30 mL butter	*Sauté lobster meat in oil and butter in a skillet for approximately 3 minutes until meat turns white.*
2 tbsp./30 mL brandy	*Add brandy to skillet and heat for approximately 1 minute.*
	Add contents of skillet to pot and stir in.
1/2 cup/125 mL whipping cream, whipped 1 tbsp./15 mL finely chopped fresh parsley	*Ladle soup into individual bowls and serve with a dollop of whipped cream in the middle of each bowl. Sprinkle with parsley and serve immediately.*

OYSTER SOUP
WITH A JULIENNE OF VEGETABLES
Zuppa di Ostriche Fantasia

Serves 6

3/4 lb./350 g fresh oysters, shucked — 10-12 oysters	*Cut oyster meat in quarters and put in a bowl. Set aside.*
2 firm, ripe tomatoes, eyes removed and scored ''x'' on top	*Blanch tomatoes in a pot of rapidly boiling water for 20 seconds, then plunge into a pot of cold water to stop the cooking. Peel, seed and julienne tomatoes. Set aside.*
1 small onion, peeled and diced 1 tbsp./15 mL butter	*Sauté onion in butter in a pot for 2-3 minutes until soft and transparent.*
2 small cloves of garlic, peeled and finely chopped	*Add garlic to pot and stir in.*
1 cup/250 mL dry white wine	*Add white wine to pot and stir in. Bring contents of pot to a boil, reduce heat and simmer for approximately 3 minutes until reduced by one-half.*
2 cups/500 mL whipping cream	*Add cream to pot and blend in. Bring contents of pot to a boil, reduce heat and simmer for approximately 10 minutes until liquid has reduced by one-third.*
2 cups/500 mL white wine sauce *(see p. 12)* — thin consistency	*Gradually add white wine sauce to pot and blend in, stirring until mixture is smooth. Simmer over low heat for 5-7 minutes until mixture is thick enough to coat the back of a spoon.*
	Add julienned tomatoes to pot and stir in.
	Add oysters to pot and heat for 1-2 minutes. Set pot aside and keep warm.

(cont'd on p. 35)

Photo #1 *(page 33):* Appetizers. *Clockwise from left:* Tomatoes Stuffed with Seafood Served with Fresh Mint; Mussels, Prawns, Scallops, Squid and Hot Red Chili Peppers Marinated in White Wine, Lemon Juice, Garlic and Fresh Herbs; Cod Seviche with Lime Juice, Olives and Fresh Herbs; Fish Pâté; and Shrimp and Zucchini Tart. Platters, bowls, plates and service courtesy of Georg Jensen.

1 small carrot, peeled and julienned 1 stalk of celery, washed, threaded, and julienned 1 leek, washed and julienned — use only the white part 1 tbsp./15 mL butter 1 tbsp./15 mL dry white wine	*Sauté carrot, celery and leek in butter and white wine in a skillet for 1-2 minutes, then add to soup in pot and stir in.*
1/2 lemon, sectioned, seeded and diced — in very small chunks	*Add chunks of lemon to pot and stir in.*
dash of Worcestershire sauce dash of Tabasco sauce	*Add Worcestershire sauce and Tabasco sauce to pot and blend in.*
1/8 tsp./pinch of finely chopped fresh basil 1/8 tsp./pinch of fresh thyme salt *(to taste)* white pepper *(to taste)*	*Season with basil, thyme, salt and pepper.*
	Ladle soup into individual bowls and serve immediately.

Photo #2 *(page 34):* Soups. *Clockwise from top:* Cream of Mussel Soup; Lobster Bisque; and Herb and Vegetable Soup with Scampi. Plates, bowls and service courtesy of Georg Jensen.

WEST COAST FISH STEW
WITH ONIONS AND TOMATOES
Cioppino al Modo Mio

Serves 6

1/2 lb./250 g fresh squid — 3-4 squid	*Clean squid by pulling off the head and pulling out the entrails. Discard head and entrails. Remove quill from squid and discard. Lay squid on a cutting board or flat surface and, using a sharp knife, scrape the membrane off. Rinse squid thoroughly under cold running water. Cut off tentacles in front of eyes and reserve. Make sure beak-like mouth is discarded. Chop tentacles, if large. Chop body into 1/2 inch/1 cm rounds. Pat squid dry with a cloth or paper towel. Set aside.*
1/2 lb./250 g fresh clams, washed and cleaned 1/2 lb./250 g fresh mussels, washed and cleaned 1/2 lb./250 g fresh crab claws, cracked 1/2 lb./250 g fresh prawn tails — shells left on	*Put clams, mussels, crab claws and prawns in a bowl and set aside.*
1/2 lb./250 g fillet of fresh cod, bones removed — cut into 2 inch/5 cm pieces 1/2 lb./250 g fillet of fresh red snapper, bones removed — cut into 2 inch/5 cm pieces 1/2 lb./250 g fillet of fresh salmon, skin and bones removed — cut into 2 inch/5 cm pieces	*Put cod, red snapper and salmon in a bowl and set aside.*
6 firm, ripe tomatoes, eyes removed and scored ''x'' on top	*Blanch tomatoes in a pot of rapidly boiling water for 20 seconds, then plunge into a pot of cold water to stop the cooking. Peel, seed and chop tomatoes. Set aside.*
1 large onion, peeled and finely chopped 2 tbsp./30 mL olive oil 2 tbsp./30 mL butter	*Sauté onion in oil and butter in a pot for 2-3 minutes until soft and transparent.*
5 cloves of garlic, peeled and finely chopped	*Add garlic to pot and stir in.*

4 fillets of anchovy, washed and chopped	*Add anchovies to pot and stir in.*
1 cup/250 mL dry white wine	*Add white wine to pot and stir in. Simmer for approximately 2 minutes.*
2 cups/500 mL cold water 2-3 cups/500-750 mL fish stock *(see p. 8)*	*Add water and fish stock to pot and blend in.*
	Add tomatoes to pot and stir in.
juice of 1 lemon	*Add lemon juice to pot and blend in.*
1 tbsp./15 mL finely chopped fresh parsley 2 tsp./10 mL finely chopped fresh basil 1 tsp./5 mL finely chopped fresh oregano 1 tsp./5 mL fresh thyme salt *(to taste)* freshly ground black pepper *(to taste)*	*Season with parsley, basil, oregano, thyme, bay leaves, salt and pepper.*
	Add squid to pot and cook for approximately 2 minutes.
	Add clams, mussels, crab claws and prawns to pot and cook for approximately 2 mintues.
	Add cod, red snapper and salmon to pot and cook, stirring occasionally, for approximately 7 minutes.
salt *(to taste)* freshly ground black pepper *(to taste)*	*Taste and adjust seasoning with salt and pepper.*
6 slices of fried bread *(see p. 28)* 1 tbsp./15 mL extra virgin olive oil 1 tbsp./15 mL finely chopped fresh parsley	*Put fried bread in the bottom of individual soup bowls. Drizzle with olive oil and sprinkle with parsley.*
	Ladle soup over bread in bowls and serve immediately.

COLD CRAB SALAD
Granchio Freddo con Limone

Serves 4

1 lb./500 g fresh crabmeat
—reserving the meat of 4 crab claws
for garnish
juice of 1/4 lemon
zest of 1/4 lemon
2 stalks of celery, washed,
threaded and very finely diced
1/2 cup/125 mL mayonnaise *(see p. 14)*
2 tbsp./30 mL chopped fresh chives
1 tbsp./15 mL fresh lemon thyme

Put crabmeat, lemon juice, lemon zest, celery, mayonnaise, chives and lemon thyme in a bowl and gently mix together.

1 head of butter or Boston lettuce,
washed and dried

Make a bed of lettuce on 4 individual plates or in 4 glass serving dishes.

meat of 4 crab claws *(reserved above)*
4 sprigs of fresh lemon thyme
1 lemon, cut into 4 wedges

Spoon crab mixture on top of lettuce. Garnish each salad with the meat of 1 crab claw and 1 sprig of lemon thyme. Garnish plates or dishes with lemon wedges and serve immediately.

COLD LOBSTER AND FRUIT SALAD
Astaco Bella Vista

Serves 4

4 (1 lb./500 g) fresh lobsters 24 cups/6 L cold water 4 tbsp./60 mL salt	*Cook lobsters in a pot of rapidly boiling salted water for 10-12 minutes, then remove lobsters from pot and cool under cold running water. Cut off claws and, using the flat side of a large kitchen knife, crack and remove meat from claws. Chop meat into 1/2 inch/1 cm pieces and set aside. Twist and pull tail away from body. Using scissors, cut the underside of tail. Remove meat from tail and slice in rounds. Set aside. Discard lobster carcass.*
1/4 honeydew melon, seeded and cut into 1/2-1 inch/1-2 cm cubes — rind removed 1 papaya, peeled, seeded and cut into 1/2-1 inch/1-2 cm cubes 1 mango, peeled, pitted and cut into 1/2-1 inch/1-2 cm cubes 1 green apple, peeled, cored and cut into 1/2-1 inch/1-2 cm cubes	*Put honeydew, papaya, mango and apple in a bowl and gently mix together.*
juice of 1/2 lime	*Sprinkle with lime juice.*
1 pink grapefruit, cut in half, seeded and sectioned	*Add grapefruit sections to bowl and gently mix together. Be careful not to break grapefruit. Set bowl aside.*
1/2 head of curly endive, washed and dried	*Arrange curly endive on 4 individual plates.*
sherry yogurt dressing *(see below)* 4 sprigs of fresh mint or fresh lemon balm	*Spoon fruit mixture on top of curly endive. Arrange lobster meat on top of fruit. Pour dressing over all. Garnish each salad with 1 sprig of mint or lemon balm and serve immediately.*

Sherry Yogurt Dressing:

2 tbsp./30 mL dry sherry 1 1/2 cups/375 mL yogurt juice of 1 orange juice of 1/2 lemon 1 tbsp./15 mL honey 1 1/2 tbsp./20 mL finely chopped fresh mint salt *(to taste)* white pepper *(to taste)*	*Mix sherry, yogurt, orange juice, lemon juice, honey, mint, salt and pepper together in a bowl.*

COLD RICE AND SEAFOOD SALAD
Frutti di Mare con Riso Freddo

Serves 4

1 shallot, peeled and finely chopped
1 tbsp./15 mL butter

Sauté shallot in butter in a pot for 1-2 minutes until soft and transparent.

1 1/4 cups/300 mL long grain white rice

Add rice to pot and gently stir to coat with butter.

1 3/4 cups/425 mL cold water

Add water to pot.

1 tbsp./15 mL butter
1/2 tsp./2 mL salt
1 bay leaf

Add butter, salt and bay leaf to pot.

Bring water to a boil. Stir rice once. Reduce heat, cover pot and cook rice for appoximately 18 minutes or until done.

Remove bay leaf from pot. Set pot aside and allow rice to cool.

1/4 lb./125 g cooked fillet of fresh salmon, skin and bones removed — cut into 1 inch/2 cm pieces
1/4 lb./125 g fresh crabmeat
1/2 lb./250 g fresh shrimp
1/4 lb./125 g cooked fresh scallops — halved, if large
1/2 lb./250 g peeled and deveined cooked fresh prawns

Put salmon, crabmeat, shrimp, scallops and prawns in a bowl and, using a wooden spoon, gently mix together.

Add rice to bowl and gently mix together.

salt *(to taste)*
freshly ground black pepper *(to taste)*

Season with salt and pepper.

dressing *(see below)*

Pour dressing over top of rice and seafood mixture in bowl and, using a wooden spoon, gently mix together. Serve immediately. Serve directly from bowl to individual plates.

Dressing:

1/4 cup/50 mL olive oil
2 tsp./10 mL vegetable oil
4 tbsp./60 mL rice vinegar
juice of 1/2 lemon
1 small red pepper, seeded
and finely chopped
4 scallions, washed and chopped
3 tbsp./45 mL toasted pine nuts
3 tbsp./45 mL finely chopped
fresh parsley

Mix olive oil, vegetable oil, rice vinegar, lemon juice, red pepper, scallions, pine nuts and parsley together in a bowl.

Do not use leftover rice in this recipe. Do not cook rice ahead — make rice fresh.

COLD SQUID SALAD
Insalatina di Calameretti

Serves 4

1 1/2 lbs./700 g fresh squid
— 12 squid

Clean squid by pulling off the head and pulling out the entrails. Discard head and entrails. Remove quill from squid and discard. Lay squid on a cutting board or flat surface and, using a sharp knife, scrape the membrane off. Rinse squid thoroughly under cold running water. Cut off tentacles in front of eyes and reserve. Make sure beak-like mouth is discarded. Chop tentacles, if large. Chop body into 1/2 inch/1 cm rounds. Pat squid dry with a cloth or paper towel. Set aside.

1/2 lb./250 g sea asparagus

Soak sea asparagus in a pot of cold water for 1 hour, then drain pot. Blanch sea asparagus in a pot of rapidly boiling water for 30 seconds-1 minute, then drain pot and freshen sea asparagus in a pot of cold water. Remove sea asparagus from this pot and drain on a cloth or paper towel. Set aside.

salt *(to taste)*
freshly ground black pepper *(to taste)*

Season squid with salt and pepper.

(cont'd over)

1/4 cup/50 mL vegetable oil	*Sauté squid in oil in a skillet for 5-7 minutes until tender and lightly golden, then remove from skillet and drain on paper towels. Set squid aside and allow to cool.*
1/2 medium onion, peeled and diced 3 tbsp./45 mL olive oil	*Sauté onion in oil in a skillet for 2-3 minutes until soft and transparent.*
1/4 tsp./1 mL peeled and finely chopped garlic	*Add garlic to skillet and sauté for approximately 1 minute, then set skillet aside.*
3 firm, ripe tomatoes, eyes removed and scored ''x'' on top	*Blanch tomatoes in a pot of rapidly boiling water for 20 seconds, then plunge into a pot of cold water to stop the cooking. Peel, seed and chop tomatoes. Put tomatoes in a blender.*
	Add onion and garlic from skillet to blender and purée.
4 tbsp./60 mL extra virgin olive oil 1 1/2 tbsp./20 mL white wine vinegar 2 tbsp./30 mL finely chopped fresh basil 1 tbsp./15 mL finely chopped fresh parsley	*Add olive oil, wine vinegar, basil and parsley to blender and mix together.*
salt *(to taste)* freshly ground black pepper *(to taste)*	*Season with salt and pepper.*
2 tbsp./30 mL marinated sundried tomatoes, drained and chopped	*Arrange sea asparagus on 4 individual plates. Put squid on top of sea asparagus. Pour tomato purée over top of squid. Garnish each salad with sundried tomatoes and serve immediately.*

FRESH MUSSEL
AND MOZZARELLA SALAD
Insalata di Cozze Caprese

Serves 4

3-4 balls of fresh Mozzarella cheese

Cut balls of Mozzarella cheese into slices and set aside.

1 lb./500 g fresh mussels,
washed and cleaned
1/4 cup/50 mL dry white wine
1/2 tsp./2 mL peeled and
finely chopped garlic

Put mussels in a pot with white wine and garlic. Cover pot and steam mussels for 3-4 minutes until they open. Drain pot and remove mussels from shells or leave them in the half-shell. Set aside.

1/2 head of radicchio,
washed and julienned
— approx. 1 1/2 cups/375 mL

Arrange radicchio on one-half of a platter.

2 cups/500 mL washed and julienned
Swiss chard

Arrange Swiss chard on other half of platter.

Put slices of Mozzarella cheese on top of radicchio — white on purple. Put mussels, in or out of the shell, on top of Swiss chard — black on green.

1/4 cup/50 mL extra virgin olive oil

Drizzle olive oil over all.

juice of 1 lemon
2 tbsp./30 mL finely chopped
fresh basil
freshly ground black pepper *(to taste)*
4 slices of lightly toasted or grilled
French or sourdough bread
(to accompany)

Sprinkle with lemon juice, basil and pepper and serve immediately. Serve directly from platter to individual plates. Serve with slices of French or sourdough bread on the side.

MARINATED MACKEREL SALAD
WITH SESAME DRESSING
Insalata di Sgombro con Sesame

Serves 4

Pre-heat oven to broil/grill.

2 (12-16 oz./350-500 g) whole fresh mackerel, filleted — each in 2 halves, with the head and tail off
salt *(to taste)*
freshly ground black pepper *(to taste)*
juice of 1/2 lemon
2 tbsp./30 mL olive oil

Rinse fillets of mackerel under cold running water and pat dry with paper towels. Season with salt and pepper. Sprinkle with lemon juice. Drizzle with olive oil.

Put fillets, flesh side down, on a buttered baking tray. Put baking tray in oven and broil/grill for approximately 2 minutes per side until just done.

sesame dressing *(see below)*

Remove baking tray from oven and put fillets, skin side down, on a platter. Pour dressing over fillets.

Put platter in the refrigerator and allow mackerel to marinate in dressing for 2 hours.

2 tbsp./30 mL toasted sesame seeds
8 sprigs of fresh cilantro

Remove platter from refrigerator and sprinkle fillets of mackerel with sesame seeds. Garnish each fillet with 2 sprigs of cilantro and serve immediately. Serve directly from platter to individual plates.

Sesame Dressing:

2 tbsp./30 mL olive oil
4 tbsp./60 mL hot sesame oil
3 tbsp./45 mL white wine vinegar
1 tbsp./15 mL peeled and finely chopped shallots
2 scallions, washed and chopped
1 tsp./5 mL peeled and finely chopped fresh ginger root
salt *(to taste)*
freshly ground black pepper *(to taste)*

Mix olive oil, sesame oil, wine vinegar, shallots, scallions, ginger, salt and pepper together in a bowl.

MARINATED SCALLOP SALAD
Insalata Capesante al Cedro

Serves 4

3/4-1 lb./350-500 g large fresh scallops	*Rinse scallops under cold running water and set aside to drain. Cut each scallop into 4-5 slices and put in a bowl.*
1/4 cup/50 mL vegetable oil	*Add vegetable oil to bowl and, using a wooden spoon, gently mix to coat scallops in oil.*
juice of 3 limes zest of 1 lime 1 tbsp./15 mL sugar	*Add lime juice, lime zest and sugar to bowl and mix together.*
white pepper *(to taste)* 1/8 tsp./pinch of cayenne 2 tbsp./30 mL finely chopped fresh dill	*Season with white pepper, cayenne and dill.*
	Put bowl in the refrigerator and allow scallops to marinate in lime juice for 2-3 hours.
	Remove bowl from refrigerator and set aside.
1 head of butter or Boston lettuce, washed and dried	*Make lettuce leaf cups on 4 individual plates and set aside.*
1 large firm, ripe tomato, eye removed and scored "x" on top	*Blanch tomato in a pot of rapidly boiling water for 20 seconds, then plunge into a pot of cold water to stop the cooking. Peel, seed and julienne tomato.*
	Add tomato to scallops in bowl and gently mix together.
1/2 long English cucumber, halved lengthwise, seeded and sliced	*Add cucumber to bowl and gently mix together.*
1 lime, cut into 4 wedges	*Using a slotted spoon, spoon scallop-tomato-cucumber mixture into lettuce leaf cups. Garnish plates with lime wedges and serve immediately.*

TUNA AND ONION SALAD
Tonno sott' Olio con Cipollina Fresca

Serves 4

2 (6 1/2 oz./184 g) tins of chunk light tuna, drained and broken into pieces — not crumbled

Put tuna in a bowl.

3 tbsp./45 mL peeled and chopped red onion
3 tbsp./45 mL peeled and chopped sweet white onion

Add red and white onion to bowl and gently mix together. Set aside.

1/3 lb./150 g fresh green beans, stemmed
8 cups/2 L cold water
1 tsp./5 mL salt

Blanch green beans in a pot of rapidly boiling salted water for approximately 5 minutes until tender-crisp, then plunge into a pot of cold water to stop the cooking. Cut beans into 1 inch/2 cm pieces and put in a bowl. Set aside.

2 firm, ripe tomatoes, eyes removed and scored "x" on top

Blanch tomatoes in a pot of rapidly boiling water for 20 seconds, then plunge into a pot of cold water to stop the cooking. Peel, seed and chop tomatoes into 1 inch/2 cm pieces.

Add tomatoes to beans in bowl and gently mix together.

2 tbsp./30 mL olive oil
2 tbsp./30 mL vegetable oil
juice of 1 lemon
1 tbsp./15 mL white wine vinegar
2 scallions, washed and chopped
salt *(to taste)*
freshly ground black pepper *(to taste)*

Mix olive oil, vegetable oil, lemon juice, vinegar, scallions, salt and pepper together in a bowl and pour over beans and tomatoes in bowl.

Add beans and tomatoes to tuna and onions in bowl and gently mix together.

1/2 head of curly endive, washed and dried
1 head of Belgian endive, washed and dried
1 bunch of watercress, washed, dried and stemmed

Arrange curly endive in the middle of a platter. Arrange Belgian endive and watercress around the edges of the platter. Put tuna-onion-bean-tomato mixture on top of curly endive in middle of platter and serve immediately. Serve directly from platter to individual plates.

WARM LOBSTER SALAD
WITH APPLE AND PAPAYA
Insalata d' Astaco con Mele e Papaya

Serves 4

4 (1 lb./500 g) fresh lobsters

Using a large kitchen knife, kill lobsters by splitting head in half lengthwise. Cut off claws and, using the flat side of knife, crack and remove meat from claws. Chop meat into 1/2 inch/1 cm pieces and set aside. Twist and pull tail away from body. Using scissors, cut the underside of tail down the centre. Remove meat from tail and slice in rounds. Set aside. Discard lobster carcass.

1/4 cup/50 mL olive oil

Sauté lobster meat in oil in a skillet for approximately 2 minutes.

1 green apple,
peeled, cored and julienned
1 tsp./5 mL peeled and
finely chopped fresh ginger root

Add apple and ginger to skillet and toss to heat.

1 papaya, peeled, seeded
and cut into 1/2 inch/1 cm cubes
1/4 cup/50 mL vegetable oil
2 tbsp./30 mL olive oil
2 tbsp./30 mL rice vinegar
1 tbsp./15 mL balsamic vinegar
1/4 tsp./1 mL peeled and
finely chopped garlic
1/8 tsp./pinch of seeded and finely
chopped hot red chili pepper
salt *(to taste)*
freshly ground black pepper *(to taste)*

Add papaya to skillet, then add vegetable oil, olive oil, rice vinegar, balsamic vinegar, garlic, chili pepper, salt and pepper and bring to a boil. Remove from heat, set aside and keep warm.

3/4 lb./350 g rice noodles
— or 1/3 lb./150 g fresh bean sprouts
2 tbsp./30 mL vegetable oil
(for rice noodles only)

Blanch rice noodles in a pot of rapidly boiling water for approximately 2 minutes until soft, then drain in a colander. Add oil to noodles in a bowl — or blanch bean sprouts in a pot of rapidly boiling water for 20 seconds, then plunge into a pot of cold water to stop the cooking. Put bean sprouts in a bowl.

(cont'd over)

1/2 long English cucumber, halved lengthwise, seeded and thinly sliced

Add cucumber to rice noodles or bean sprouts in bowl and gently mix together.

Transfer contents of bowl to a platter and arrange neatly.

Spoon lobster-apple-papaya mixture in skillet over cucumber-rice noodle or cucumber-bean sprout mixture on platter and serve immediately. Serve directly from platter to individual plates.

WARM PRAWN SALAD WITH THREE LETTUCES
Gamberoni con Tre Insalata

Serves 4

1 lb./500 g fresh jumbo prawns, peeled and deveined — if prawns have eggs, reserve when peeling and add to dressing

Rinse prawns under cold running water and set aside to drain. Cut prawns in half lengthwise, then in half crosswise. Set aside.

2 heads of butter or Boston lettuce, washed and dried — or 1 head of romaine lettuce, washed and dried 1-1 1/2 heads of Belgian endive, washed and dried 1 head of red oak leaf lettuce, washed and dried — or 1 head of arugula, washed and dried — or 1 1/2 cups/375 mL washed and dried, 2 inch/5 cm pieces of Swiss chard

Tear lettuces (if not already torn) into 2 inch/5 cm pieces and arrange on a platter. Set aside.

4 tbsp./60 mL extra virgin olive oil

Quickly sauté prawns in oil in a skillet for approximately 30 seconds.

juice of 1/2 lemon
2 tbsp./30 mL balsamic vinegar
prawn eggs
(reserved above — if available)
salt *(to taste)*
white pepper *(to taste)*

Add lemon juice, balsamic vinegar, prawn eggs (if available), salt and pepper to skillet, stir, then pour contents of skillet over lettuces on platter and serve immediately. Serve directly from platter to individual plates.

Freshwater Fish

ARCTIC CHAR
Salmerino

Background: *Arctic char are saltwater fish that have become landlocked. They are found in arctic and alpine areas of the world and are classified as freshwater fish. They have elongated bodies, similar to salmon and trout, but they have finer scales and teeth. They are silvery in colour, with deep blue or greenish blue on their backs and upper sides, and they have a series of small pink dots along and below their lateral lines. Char are high in fat content and have a very delicate flavour. The colour of their flesh varies according to their diet. They are often fished by the Inuit from short rivers along the Arctic coast of Canada. Since relatively few fish are available to be caught, Arctic char are not widely available in the marketplace. They are available fresh and frozen all year round, though they are available fresh, for the most part, in the summer.*

STEAMED ARCTIC CHAR
WRAPPED IN ROMAINE LETTUCE   *Serves 4*
Salmerino Lesso con Lattuga

4 (6 oz./175 g) fillets of fresh Arctic char
salt *(to taste)*
white pepper *(to taste)*
juice of 1/2 lemon
flour *(to dust)*

Rinse fillets of Arctic char under cold running water and pat dry with paper towels. Season with salt and pepper. Sprinkle with lemon juice. Dust with flour.

3 tbsp./45 mL vegetable oil

Sear char in hot oil and butter in a skillet, then remove from skillet and set aside.

4 large leaves of romaine lettuce, washed and dried
4 cups/1 L cold water
1 tsp./5 mL salt

Blanch leaves of lettuce in a pot of rapidly boiling salted water for 10 seconds, then plunge into a pot of cold water to stop the cooking. Drain pot and put lettuce leaves on paper towels to dry, then trim the core of each leaf.

(cont'd over)

Put lettuce leaves, face side down, on a flat surface and put fillets of Arctic char on top of leaves.

Wrap char in lettuce leaves and carefully put in a buttered baking pan large enough to contain fish.

Pre-heat oven to 375°F/190°C.

1/2 cup/125 mL dry white vermouth

Add vermouth to baking pan and bring to a boil on top of the stove.

buttered paper

Cover baking pan with a sheet of buttered paper. Put pan in oven and steam for 10-12 minutes, then remove pan from oven and put lettuce-wrapped char on a platter. Set platter aside and keep warm. Reserve liquid in pan and transfer to a saucepan. Simmer until liquid has reduced by one-half.

1/2 cup/125 mL whipping cream

Add cream to saucepan and blend in. Bring to a boil, reduce heat and simmer for approximately 2 minutes.

2 tbsp./30 mL butter

Add butter to saucepan and blend in.

1 tsp./5 mL freshly squeezed lemon juice

Add lemon juice to saucepan and blend in.

salt *(to taste)*
white pepper *(to taste)*

Season with salt and pepper.

Spoon contents of saucepan over lettuce-wrapped char on platter and serve immediately. Serve directly from platter to individual plates.

CARP
Carpio

Background: *Carp are thought to have originated in China, but they are found in Europe, Africa and North America. There is only one species of carp, but about 1,500 varieties worldwide. Carp were the first fish known to have been cultivated and they are available both wild and cultivated in North America. Carp are a favourite fish in Chinese and Italian cuisine. Carp are gold to olive brown in colour, fading to pale yellow, with red highlights and coarse scales. They are bottom-dwellers, living in warm, shallow waters of lakes, ponds and slow-moving rivers that are rich in vegetation. They range in weight from 2-3 lbs./1-1.5 kg and have moderate fat content. They have flaky, white, mild-flavoured flesh, which makes them extremely versatile in cooking. Carp are available, whole or in fillets, all year round, but are best caught wild between November and April, because, in summer, they can have a muddy flavour and can be toxic.*

PAN-FRIED FILLET OF CARP
IN TOMATO SAUCE
Serves 4
Filetto di Carpio Fritto in Padella

4 (6-8 oz./175-250 g) fillets of fresh carp
salt *(to taste)*
freshly ground black pepper *(to taste)*
1/2 cup/125 mL fresh fine white breadcrumbs — mixed with 1/4 cup/ 50 mL flour *(to coat)*

Rinse fillets of carp under cold running water and pat dry with paper towels. Season with salt and pepper. Dredge in breadcrumb-flour mixture.

1/4 cup/50 mL olive oil
2 tbsp./30 mL butter

Fry carp in oil and butter in a skillet for 4-6 minutes per side until lightly brown, then remove from skillet, set aside and keep warm.

2 cups/500 mL tomato sauce *(see p. 11)*
4 large leaves of fresh basil, julienned

Make a bed of tomato sauce on a platter. Put fillets of carp on top of tomato sauce on platter. Garnish with julienned basil and serve immediately. Serve directly from platter to individual plates.

ROAST WHOLE CARP
WITH TARRAGON
Carpio Arrosto con Dragoncello

Serves 4

1 (3 lb./1.5 kg) whole fresh carp, scaled — with the fins and gills removed	*Rinse carp under cold running water and pat dry with paper towels. Set aside.*
	Pre-heat oven to 425°F/220°C.
1/4 cup/50 mL extra virgin olive oil juice of 1 lemon 1/2 tsp./2 mL peeled and finely chopped garlic 1 tbsp./15 mL Dijon mustard 1 tbsp./15 mL finely chopped fresh parsley 1 tbsp./15 mL finely chopped fresh tarragon salt *(to taste)* white pepper *(to taste)*	*Mix olive oil, lemon juice, garlic, mustard, parsley, tarragon, salt and pepper together in a bowl and rub into carp, inside and out.*
2 sprigs of fresh tarragon	*Put sprigs of tarragon in cavity of fish.*
1 onion, peeled and chopped 1 lemon, cut into slices	*Put onion and lemon slices in the bottom of a roasting pan.*
	Put carp on top of onion and lemon slices in roasting pan. Put roasting pan in oven and roast for 10 minutes, then reduce heat to 350°F/180°C and roast for an additional 30 minutes until fish is done.
	When fish is done, remove roasting pan from oven and put carp on a platter. Set platter aside and keep warm. Reserve liquid in pan.
1/4 cup/50 mL dry white wine	*Deglaze pan with white wine.*
1/4 cup/50 mL whipping cream	*Add cream to pan and blend in. Bring to a boil, reduce heat and simmer for approximately 1 minute.*
2 tbsp./30 mL butter	*Add butter to pan and blend in.*
1 tbsp./15 mL freshly squeezed lemon juice	*Add lemon juice to pan and blend in.*

1 tbsp./15 mL finely chopped
fresh tarragon
1 tbsp./15 mL finely chopped
fresh parsley
salt *(to taste)*
white pepper *(to taste)*

*Season with tarragon, parsley, salt
and pepper.*

*Strain sauce in pan through a sieve
lined with a linen or muslin cloth into
a sauceboat and serve warm.*

*Serve carp on platter with tarragon
sauce in sauceboat on the side. Serve
immediately. Slice at the table. Serve
directly from platter to individual
plates.*

POACHED WHOLE CARP SERVED COLD
WITH GARLIC MAYONNAISE   *Serves 4*
Carpio Freddo Aioli

1 (3 lb./1.5 kg) whole fresh
carp, scaled — with the fins
and gills removed

*Rinse carp under cold running
water and pat dry with paper towels.
Set aside.*

12 cups/3 L cold water
4 thin slices of onion
— separated into rings
1 stalk of celery, washed and sliced
3 tbsp./45 mL dry white wine
3 tbsp./45 mL white vinegar
1 tsp./5 mL crushed
white peppercorns
2 bay leaves
2 sprigs of fresh parsley
1/4 tsp./1 mL crushed coriander
1 sprig of fresh thyme

*Make a court bouillon by putting
water, onion, celery, white wine,
vinegar, peppercorns, bay leaves,
parsley, coriander and thyme in a pot
and bringing to a boil. Reduce
heat to a simmer.*

*Put carp in court bouillon and poach
for 10-12 minutes, then remove carp
from pot. Set carp aside to drain and
cool.*

1-1 1/2 cups/250-375 mL garlic
mayonnaise *(see p. 13)*

*Put carp on a platter and serve cold
with garlic mayonnaise in a bowl on
the side. Slice at the table. Serve
directly from platter to individual
plates.*

CATFISH
Siluro

Background: *Catfish, until recently, were best-known in the regional cuisine of the American Deep South and were not highly prized because they were often thought to have a muddy flavour. Cultivation has changed all of that and catfish are in the process of becoming an enormously popular freshwater fish, sought after for their delicate flavour and their fine-textured, lean, light-coloured flesh, which is firm and flaky. There are several species of catfish, but the best-known are the channel or blue catfish, which range in weight from 1-3 lbs./500 g-1.5 kg, and the bullhead, which average approximately 1 lb./500 g in weight. Wild catfish are much larger. Catfish that have been cultivated are available fresh, whole or in fillets, all year round, but the demand for them far exceeds the supply, so they are not always available, especially beyond the restaurant trade. Freshwater catfish is not to be confused with Atlantic catfish, also known as ocean catfish, Atlantic wolffish, striped wolffish or ocean wolffish, which is also edible, and which is available in Eastern Canadian markets.*

PAN-FRIED FILLET OF CATFISH
WITH AROMATIC OIL
Serves 4
Filetti di Siluro con Olio Erbe Fini-Peperoncino

4 (6-8 oz./175-250 g) fillets of fresh catfish
salt *(to taste)*
freshly ground black pepper *(to taste)*
1/8 tsp./pinch of cayenne
juice of 1/2 lemon
flour *(to dust)*

Rinse fillets of catfish under cold running water and pat dry with paper towels. Season with salt, black pepper and cayenne. Sprinkle with lemon juice. Dust with flour.

1/4 cup/50 mL peanut oil
2 tbsp./30 mL butter

Fry catfish in oil and butter in a skillet for 3-4 minutes per side until golden brown, then remove from skillet and drain on paper towels.

aromatic oil *(see below)*

Put fillets of catfish on a platter. Pour aromatic oil over fillets of catfish on platter and serve immediately. Serve directly from platter to individual plates.

Aromatic Oil:

1/2 cup/125 mL extra virgin olive oil
juice of 1/2 lemon
1/4 tsp./1 mL peeled and
finely chopped garlic
1/2 tsp./2 mL finely chopped
fresh parsley
1 tbsp./15 mL finely chopped
fresh basil
1/4 tsp./1 mL finely chopped
fresh cilantro
1/4 tsp./1 mL finely chopped
fresh dill
1/2 tsp./2 mL finely chopped
fresh tarragon
1/2 tsp./2 mL fresh thyme
salt *(to taste)*
freshly ground black pepper *(to taste)*

Mix olive oil, lemon juice, garlic, parsley, basil, cilantro, dill, tarragon, thyme, salt and pepper together in a bowl and set aside. Make aromatic oil at least 1 hour in advance of cooking recipe above.

PAN-FRIED FILLET OF CATFISH WITH RAISIN SAUCE
Filetti di Siluro con Uva Secca

Serves 4

4 (6-8 oz./175-250 g) fillets of
fresh catfish
salt *(to taste)*
white pepper *(to taste)*
juice of 1/2 lemon
flour *(to dust)*

Rinse fillets of catfish under cold running water and pat dry with paper towels. Season with salt, white pepper and cayenne. Sprinkle with lemon juice. Dust with flour.

1/4 cup/50 mL peanut oil
1 tbsp./15 mL butter

Fry catfish in oil and butter in a skillet for 3-4 minutes per side until golden brown, then remove from skillet and drain on paper towels. Put fillets on a platter, set aside and keep warm.

1/4 cup/50 mL golden seedless raisins
2 tbsp./30 mL grappa
2 tbsp./30 mL dry white wine
juice of 1/2 lemon
salt *(to taste)*
white pepper *(to taste)*

Add raisins, grappa, white wine, lemon juice, salt and pepper to skillet and and simmer for 1-2 minutes.

Spoon contents of skillet over fillets of catfish on platter and serve immediately. Serve directly from platter to individual plates.

SAUTEED FILLET OF CATFISH FLAMED
WITH VODKA
Serves 4
Filetti di Siluro alla Moda di Mosca

4 (6-8 oz./175-250 g) fillets of fresh catfish salt *(to taste)* freshly ground black pepper *(to taste)* 1/8 tsp./pinch of cayenne juice of 1/2 lemon flour *(to dust)*	*Rinse fillets of catfish under cold running water and pat dry with paper towels. Season with salt, black pepper and cayenne. Sprinkle with lemon juice. Dust with flour.*
1/4 cup/50 mL peanut oil	*Sauté catfish in oil in a skillet for 3-4 minutes per side until golden brown, then drain oil from skillet. Leave fillets in skillet.*
1 tbsp./15 mL vodka	*Add vodka to skillet and flambé.*
	When flame dies down, remove fillets from skillet and put on a platter. Set aside and keep warm.
2 slices of bacon, finely chopped	*Add bacon to skillet and cook until crisp.*
1 stalk of celery, washed, threaded and diced — reserving the leaves for garnish 1 tbsp./15 mL peeled and finely chopped shallots	*Add celery and shallots to skillet and sauté for approximately 1 minute, then drain oil from skillet.*
2 tbsp./30 mL vodka	*Add vodka to skillet and flambé.*
3 tbsp./45 mL whipping cream	*When flame dies down, add cream to skillet and stir in.*
1/4 cup/50 mL seeded and chopped fresh tomatoes	*Add tomatoes to skillet and stir in.*
salt *(to taste)* freshly ground black pepper *(to taste)*	*Season with salt and pepper.*
leaves of celery *(reserved above)*	*Spoon contents of skillet over fillets of catfish on platter. Garnish with celery leaves and serve immediately. Serve directly from platter to individual plates.*

SAUTEED FILLET OF CATFISH
WITH BLACK BEAN SAUCE
Filetti di Siluro con Olio di Soia

Serves 4

4 (6-8 oz./175-250 g) fillets of fresh catfish
4 dashes of soy sauce
cornstarch *(to dust)*

Rinse fillets of catfish under cold running water and pat dry with paper towels. Spinkle with soy sauce. Dust with cornstarch.

1/4 cup/50 mL peanut oil

Sauté catfish in oil in a skillet for 3-4 minutes per side until golden brown, then remove from skillet and drain on paper towels. Put fillets on a platter, set aside and keep warm.

1/4 cup/50 mL black beans

Rinse black beans under cold running water and set aside to drain. Pat beans dry. Put beans in a bowl and mash or put them in a blender and purée. If using a blender, transfer purée of beans to a bowl.

1 tbsp./15 mL soy sauce
1 tbsp./15 mL dry white wine
1/2 tsp./2 mL sugar
1/8 tsp./pinch of salt

Add soy sauce, white wine, sugar and salt to bowl and blend in. Set bowl aside.

1 tbsp./15 mL peeled and finely chopped garlic
2 tbsp./30 mL peanut oil

Sauté garlic in oil in skillet for approximately 30 seconds.

Add black bean mixture in bowl to skillet and blend in. Simmer for approximately 1 minute.

1 cup/250 mL chicken stock *(see p. 00)* or cold water

Add chicken stock or water to skillet and blend in. Simmer for 2-3 minutes.

1 tbsp./15 mL cornstarch — mixed with 1 tbsp./ 15 mL cold water

Add cornstarch mixture to skillet and blend in. Simmer until sauce thickens slightly.

salt *(to taste)*
white pepper *(to taste)*

Season with salt and pepper.

Spoon contents of skillet over fillets of catfish on platter and serve immediately. Serve directly from platter to individual plates.

CRAYFISH
Gambero d'Acqua Dolce

Background: *Crayfish are small freshwater crustaceans, cousins to the lobster. They are enjoyable to eat because of their size and flavour. Crayfish are, for the most part, cultivated, but also they are found wild in rivers and estuaries throughout North America. They have long been popular in Europe and, in the southern United States, they are often used in Creole or Cajun cooking. They range in weight from 2-8 oz./50-250 g, of which only 20% is meat. Crayfish are reddish brown when alive, but they turn bright red when cooked. They are low in fat content and are available fresh, flown in from Louisiana and California, at different times of the year. They are a good fish to use for decoration because of their size. Crayfish are also known as crawfish or crawdads. They are not to be confused with spiny lobsters, which are also known as crayfish, but who live in the ocean.*

STEAMED CRAYFISH SERVED COLD
WITH MAYONNAISE
Serves 4
Gambero d' Acqua Dolce Freddo con Maionese

80 (2 oz./50 g) fresh crayfish
24 cups/6 L cold water
2 tbsp./30 mL salt

Rinse crayfish in a pot of salted water for 10 minutes, then drain pot and set crayfish aside.

1/2 medium onion, peeled and finely chopped
3 tbsp./45 mL olive oil
1 tbsp./15 mL butter

Sauté onion in oil and butter in a pot for 2-3 minutes until soft and transparent.

1/2 cup/125 mL dry white wine
1 cup/250 mL cold water

Add white wine and water to pot and stir in.

salt *(to taste)*
1/8 tsp./pinch of cayenne

Season with salt and cayenne.

Bring contents of pot to a boil. Add crayfish to pot. Cover pot and steam crayfish for approximately 2 minutes.

Using a slotted spoon, remove crayfish from pot and set aside to cool. Using hands, break off crayfish heads and discard. Gently remove meat from tails and set meat aside.

1 1/2-2 cups/375-500 mL mayonnaise
(see p. 14)

Put crayfish meat on a platter and serve cold with mayonnaise in a bowl on the side.

SAUTEED CRAYFISH
WITH MARSALA CREAM SAUCE
Gambero d' Acqua Dolce Capriccioso

Serves 4

80 (2 oz./50 g) fresh crayfish 24 cups/6 L cold water 2 tbsp./30 mL salt	*Rinse crayfish in a pot of salted water for 10 minutes, then drain pot and set crayfish aside.*
boiling water *(to cover)*	*Return crayfish to pot and cover with boiling water. Let stand for approximately 2 minutes, then, using a slotted spoon, remove crayfish from pot and set aside to cool. Using hands, break off crayfish heads and discard. Gently remove meat from tails and set meat aside.*
2 tbsp./30 mL peeled and finely chopped shallots 2 tbsp./30 mL butter	*Sauté shallots in butter in a skillet for approximately 30 seconds.*
	Add crayfish meat to skillet. Toss and heat for approximately 30 seconds.
1/4 cup/50 mL marsala wine	*Add marsala wine to skillet and flambé.*
	When flame dies down, using a slotted spoon, remove crayfish meat from skillet and set aside. Reserve liquid in skillet and simmer until reduced by one-half.
1/2 cup/125 mL whipping cream	*Add cream to skillet and blend in. Bring to a boil, reduce heat and simmer for 3-5 minutes until sauce thickens slightly.*
3-4 tbsp./45-60 mL butter	*Add butter to skillet and blend in.*
juice of 1 lemon	*Add lemon juice to skillet and blend in.*
salt *(to taste)* freshly ground black pepper *(to taste)*	*Season with salt and pepper.*
	Return crayfish meat to skillet. Toss and heat for 1-2 minutes.
	Transfer contents of skillet to a platter or individual plates and serve immediately.

LAKE BASS
Spigola

Background: *There are two different types of freshwater bass in North America: black bass and white bass. Because bass are a bony fish, they are usually filleted right away. They have firm, lean, white-coloured flesh, which flakes easily and has a delicate flavour. Bass are one of the most popular freshwater fish with sport fisherman. They are not to be confused with sea bass, which is a different fish that is widely available.*

BAKED FILLET OF LAKE BASS
WITH FOUR PEPPERCORNS
Serves 4
Filetto di Spigola al Forno con Pepe Misto

3 tsp./15 mL whole dried mixed peppercorns — 1 tsp./5 mL each of red, white and black peppercorns — plus 1 tsp./5 mL whole marinated green peppercorns, drained
4 tbsp./60 mL port

Soak peppercorns in port in a bowl in the refrigerator for several hours in advance of cooking recipe below.

Pre-heat oven to 350°F/180°C.

4 (8 oz./250 g) fillets of fresh lake bass
salt *(to taste)*
juice of 1 lemon
2 1/2 tbsp./40 mL melted butter
fresh fine white breadcrumbs
(to coat)

Rinse fillets of lake bass under cold running water and pat dry with paper towels. Season with salt. Sprinkle with lemon juice. Drizzle with butter, then roll in breadcrumbs. Press breadcrumbs onto lake bass and put in a buttered baking dish.

Put baking dish in oven and bake for approximately 10 minutes. While lake bass is baking, put peppercorns and port in a skillet and heat.

2 tbsp./30 mL fish stock *(see p. 8)*

Add fish stock to skillet and blend in.

1 tsp./5 mL freshly squeezed lemon juice

Add lemon juice to skillet and blend in. Simmer for 2-3 minutes, then remove skillet from heat.

2 tbsp./30 mL butter

Add butter to skillet and blend in.

salt *(to taste)*

Season with salt.

When lake bass has finished baking, remove baking dish from oven and put fillets on a platter. Spoon contents of skillet over fillets of lake bass on platter and serve immediately. Serve directly from platter to individual plates.

FILLET OF LAKE BASS POACHED IN MILK AND SERVED WITH MARINATED RED ONIONS *Serves 4*
Filetto di Spigola Cotto nel Latte con Cipolle

1 medium red onion, peeled and thinly sliced
3 tbsp./45 mL extra virgin olive oil
1 tbsp./15 mL white wine vinegar
1 tsp./5 mL finely chopped fresh oregano
salt *(to taste)*
white pepper *(to taste)*

Marinate onion in olive oil, wine vinegar, oregano, salt and pepper in a bowl in the refrigerator for 2 hours in advance of cooking recipe below.

4 (8 oz./250 g) fillets of fresh lake bass
salt *(to taste)*
white pepper *(to taste)*

Rinse fillets of lake bass under cold running water and pat dry with paper towels. Season with salt and pepper and set aside.

1 cup/250 mL milk
1 tbsp./15 mL butter

Put milk and butter in a baking pan and bring to a boil on top of the stove, then reduce heat.

2 thin slices of onion — separated into rings

Add onion rings to baking pan.

1 sprig of fresh oregano
1 sprig of fresh thyme
1 bay leaf

Season with oregano, thyme and bay leaf.

Add lake bass to baking pan and poach for 6-8 minutes, then remove fillets from pan and set aside to drain. Keep fillets warm.

1 tbsp./15 mL finely chopped fresh parsley

Put fillets of lake bass on a platter and top with marinated red onions. Sprinkle with parsley and serve immediately. Serve directly from platter to individual plates.

PAN-FRIED FILLET OF LAKE BASS
WITH SHRIMP MOUSSE
Serves 4
Filetto di Spigola con Crema di Gamberetti

4 (8 oz./250 g) fillets of fresh lake bass
salt *(to taste)*
white pepper *(to taste)*
juice of 1 lemon
flour *(to dust)*

Rinse fillets of lake bass under cold running water and pat dry with paper towels. Season with salt and pepper. Sprinkle with lemon juice. Dust with flour.

1/4 cup/50 mL olive oil
1 tbsp./15 mL butter

Fry lake bass in oil and butter in a skillet for 4-5 minutes per side until golden brown, then remove from skillet, put on a platter, set aside and keep warm.

shrimp mousse *(see below)*

Serve with a generous helping of shrimp mousse on top of each fillet. Serve directly from platter to individual plates.

Shrimp Mousse:

4 tbsp./60 mL butter
1/2 lb./250 g fresh shrimp
1 tsp./5 mL freshly squeezed lemon juice
dash of Worcestershire sauce
salt *(to taste)*
white pepper *(to taste)*

Put butter, shrimp, lemon juice, Worcestershire sauce, salt and pepper in a mixing bowl and whip for approximately 10 minutes until butter triples in volume. Make shrimp mousse in advance of cooking recipe above and store in refrigerator until ready to use.

If there is any leftover shrimp mousse, it may be stored in a sealed plastic container in the refrigerator for 2-3 days.

SAUTEED FILLET OF LAKE BASS FLAMED WITH RYE
Serves 4
Filetto di Spigola Canadese

4 (8 oz./250 g) fillets of fresh lake bass
salt *(to taste)*
freshly ground black pepper *(to taste)*
juice of 1/2 lemon
flour *(to dust)*

Rinse fillets of lake bass under cold running water and pat dry with paper towels. Season with salt and pepper. Sprinkle with lemon juice. Dust with flour.

1/4 cup/50 mL olive oil
1 tbsp./15 mL butter

Sauté lake bass in oil and butter in a skillet for 4-5 minutes per side until golden brown, then drain oil from skillet. Leave fillets in skillet.

2 tbsp./30 mL butter
1 tbsp./15 mL peeled and finely chopped shallots
2 1/2 tbsp./40 mL rye

Add butter and shallots to skillet, then add rye to skillet and flambé.

juice of 1/2 lemon
2 tbsp./30 mL chopped fresh chives

When flame dies down, transfer contents of skillet to a platter. Sprinkle with lemon juice and chives and serve immediately. Serve directly from platter to individual plates.

PERCH
Pesce Persico

Background: *Perch are brightly coloured, spiny-finned fish, greenish above and golden yellow below. Perch are found all over the world in freshwater lakes, ponds, rivers and streams and they are found in saltwater as well. Perch found in Canada, because of its cold waters, are thought to have the best flavour and to be of the highest quality. River perch range in weight up to 4 lbs./2 kg. Those found in lakes tend to be much smaller. Perch are low in fat content. They are delicate in flavour and are highly digestible. They are available fresh, whole or in fillets, all year round.*

BAKED ROLLED FILLET OF PERCH STUFFED WITH SPINACH AND RICOTTA CHEESE   *Serves 4*
Involtini di Pesce Persico con Spinaci

4 (6 oz./175 g) fillets of fresh perch
salt *(to taste)*
white pepper *(to taste)*

Rinse fillets of perch under cold running water and pat dry with paper towels. Gently pound fillets to flatten between two pieces of plastic wrap. Season with salt and pepper and set aside.

2 large bunches of fresh spinach, washed and stemmed

Blanch spinach in a pot of rapidly boiling water for approximately 2 minutes, then drain pot and squeeze spinach dry. Finely chop spinach and put in a bowl.

1/2 cup/125 mL Ricotta cheese

Add Ricotta cheese to bowl and mix together thoroughly.

salt *(to taste)*
white pepper *(to taste)*
1/8 tsp./pinch of ground nutmeg

Season with salt, pepper and nutmeg.

Lay each fillet on a flat work surface. Spoon spinach-Ricotta cheese mixture on top of each fillet to fill the fillet crosswise, then roll each fillet.

Put rolled fillets, seam side down, in a buttered baking dish. Set baking dish aside.

Pre-heat oven to 350°F/180°C.

1/4 cup/50 mL dry white wine
1/4 cup/50 mL fish stock *(see p. 8)*
2 tbsp./30 mL butter

*Put white wine, fish stock and butter
in a saucepan and bring to a boil.*

*Pour contents of saucepan over fillets of
perch in baking dish.*

*Put baking dish in the oven and bake
for 15-20 minutes until fish is done.*

*Remove baking dish from oven and put
fillets of perch on a platter. Set platter
aside and keep warm. Reserve liquid in
dish and transfer to a saucepan.*

1/4 cup/50 mL whipping cream
2 tbsp./30 mL butter
juice of 1/2 lemon

*Add cream, butter and lemon juice
to saucepan. Blend in and simmer
for 2-3 minutes.*

salt *(to taste)*
white pepper *(to taste)*

Season with salt and pepper.

*Strain contents of saucepan through a
fine sieve over fillets of perch on platter
and serve immediately. Serve directly
from platter to individual plates.*

BAKED WHOLE PERCH STUFFED WITH ONIONS, GARLIC, BREADCUBES AND FRESH HERBS COOKED IN GRAPEFRUIT JUICE AND SERVED WITH GRAPEFRUIT SECTIONS

Serves 4

Pesce Persico del Bongustaio

2 (3 lb./1.5 kg) whole fresh perch, scaled — with the fins and gills removed	*Rinse perch under cold running water and pat dry with paper towels. Set aside.*
1 medium onion, peeled and finely chopped 2 tbsp./30 mL olive oil 2 tbsp./30 mL vegetable oil	*Sauté onion in oil in a skillet for 2-3 minutes until soft and transparent, then put in a bowl.*
1 tsp./5 mL peeled and finely chopped garlic zest of 1/2 lemon 1 tsp./5 mL finely chopped fresh basil 1/2 tsp./2 mL finely chopped fresh oregano 1/4 tsp./1 mL chopped fresh rosemary 1 tsp./5 mL fresh thyme	*Add garlic, lemon zest, basil, oregano, rosemary and thyme to bowl and mix together.*
3 cups/750 mL day-old white breadcubes — 1/4 inch/6 mm cubes	*Add breadcubes to bowl and mix together.*
1 egg 3 tbsp./45 mL Béchamel sauce *(see p. 8)*	*Add egg and Béchamel sauce to bowl and mix together thoroughly.*
salt *(to taste)* white pepper *(to taste)*	*Season with salt and pepper.*
	Pre-heat oven to 400°F/200°C.
	Stuff cavity of each perch with breadcube stuffing and put fish in a buttered baking pan.
1/4 cup/50 mL freshly squeezed grapefruit juice	*Pour grapefruit juice over fish in baking pan.*
2 tbsp./30 mL olive oil	*Drizzle fish with olive oil.*

(cont'd on p. 69)

Photo #3 *(page 67):* Salads. *Clockwise from foreground:* Cold Squid Salad; Warm Lobster Salad with Apple and Papaya; and Fresh Mussel and Mozzarella Salad. Platters and bowl courtesy of Georg Jensen.

*Put baking pan in the oven and bake
for 25-35 minutes until fish are done.*

8 sections of pink grapefruit,
peeled and seeded
extra virgin olive oil *(to coat)*

*When fish are done, remove baking
pan from oven and transfer perch
to a platter. Garnish each fish with
4 sections of grapefruit and drizzle olive
oil over fish. Serve immediately. Slice
at the table. Serve directly from platter
to individual plates.*

PAN-FRIED FILLET OF PERCH
WITH ALMONDS AND PARSLEY   *Serves 4*
Filetti di Pesce Persico con Mandorla

4 (6-8 oz./175-250 g) fillets of fresh
perch
salt *(to taste)*
freshly ground black pepper *(to taste)*
juice of 1 lemon
flour *(to dust)*

*Rinse fillets of perch under cold
running water and pat dry with paper
towels. Season with salt and pepper.
Sprinkle with lemon juice. Dust
with flour.*

1/4 cup/50 mL olive oil
1 tbsp./15 mL butter

*Fry perch in oil and butter in a
skillet for 4-6 minutes per side until
golden brown, then remove from skillet,
put on a platter, set aside and keep
warm. Drain oil from skillet.*

3 tbsp./45 mL butter

Melt butter in skillet.

juice of 1 lemon
1-2 dashes of Worcestershire sauce

*Add lemon juice and Worcestershire
sauce to skillet and blend in.*

5 tbsp./75 mL toasted sliced almonds
1 tbsp./15 mL finely chopped
fresh parsley

*Add almonds and parsley to skillet
and stir until almonds are coated
in butter and parsley.*

*Spoon contents of skillet over fillets
of perch on platter and serve immediately.
Serve directly from platter to individual
plates.*

Photo #4 *(page 68)*: Freshwater Fish.   *Clockwise from top:* Sautéed Crayfish with Marsala
Cream Sauce; Steamed Arctic Char Wrapped in Romaine Lettuce; and Quenelles of Pike in
White Wine-Sorrel Sauce. Casseroles *(right and foreground)* courtesy of Georg Jensen.

FILLET OF PERCH BRAISED IN ZINFANDEL
WITH TOMATOES
Filetti di Pesce Persico Brasato allo Zinfandel

Serves 4

4 (6-8 oz./175-250 g) fillets of fresh perch	*Rinse fillets of perch under cold running water and pat dry with paper towels. Put in a buttered baking pan and set aside.*
6 firm, ripe tomatoes, eyes removed and scored "x" on top	*Blanch tomatoes in a pot of rapidly boiling water for 20 seconds, then plunge into a pot of cold water to stop the cooking. Peel, seed and chop tomatoes into 2 inch/5 cm wedges. Set tomatoes aside.*
1/2 medium onion, peeled and finely chopped 3 tbsp./45 mL olive oil	*Sauté onion in oil in a skillet for 2-3 minutes until soft and transparent.*
1/4 tsp./1 mL peeled and finely chopped garlic	*Add garlic to skillet and sauté for approximately 1 minute.*
	Add tomatoes to skillet and stir in.
1/4 cup/50 mL zinfandel wine	*Add zinfandel to skillet and stir in.*
1 sprig of fresh oregano 1 sprig of fresh thyme salt *(to taste)* freshly ground black pepper *(to taste)*	*Season with oregano, thyme, salt and pepper.*
	Bring contents of skillet to a boil, then pour over fillets of perch in baking pan.
	Pre-heat oven to 375°F/190°C.
	Put baking pan in oven and braise for 8-10 minutes.
4 sprigs of fresh thyme 1 lemon, cut into 4 wedges	*Remove baking pan from oven and transfer contents of pan to a platter. Garnish each fillet of perch with 1 sprig of thyme. Garnish platter with lemon wedges and serve immediately. Serve directly from platter to individual plates.*

PICKEREL
Sandra

Background: *Pickerel and pike are used interchangeably. Pickerel have gold colouring and flat, glass-like eyes. These characteristics give pickerel a number of names. They are variously known as: walleye, yellow pickerel, walleye pike, yellow pike, jackfish, golden pike, opal eye and doré. Pickerel are smaller than pike and not as oddly shaped. They have firm, snowy-white flesh that has a sweet flavour. They are low in fat content and are available fresh, whole or in fillets, all year round.*

BAKED WHOLE PICKEREL BRAISED IN ROSE WINE WITH MINT LEAVES
Serves 4
Sandra Brasato con Menta Salsa Rosa

1 (2-3 lb./1-1.5 kg) whole fresh pickerel, scaled — with the fins and gills removed
salt *(to taste)*
freshly ground black pepper *(to taste)*
2 tbsp./30 mL white wine vinegar
4 tbsp./60 mL finely chopped fresh mint

Rinse pickerel under cold running water and pat dry with paper towels. Season with salt and pepper and put in a buttered baking pan. Sprinkle with wine vinegar and mint.

2 cups/500 mL rosé wine
1/4 onion, peeled and finely chopped
1 medium carrot, peeled and finely chopped
1 stalk of celery, washed and finely chopped
1 clove of garlic, peeled and finely chopped
4 tbsp./60 mL finely chopped fresh mint
1 bay leaf
1 sprig of fresh thyme
1 tbsp./15 mL sugar

Put rosé wine, onion, carrot, celery, garlic, mint, bay leaf, thyme and sugar in baking pan around pickerel.

Pre-heat oven to 400°F/200°C

Put baking pan in oven and braise for 10 minutes, then reduce heat to 300°F/150°C and braise for an additional 20 minutes until fish is done.

(cont'd over)

	Remove baking pan from oven and put pickerel on a platter. Set aside and keep warm. Reserve liquid in pan.
2 tbsp./30 mL whipping cream	*Add cream to pan and blend in. Simmer for approximately 2 minutes.*
4 tbsp./60 mL butter	*Add butter to pan and blend in.*
	Strain sauce in pan through a sieve lined with a linen or muslin cloth into a sauceboat.
sprigs of fresh mint	*Garnish pickerel on platter with sprigs of mint and serve with mint-rosé wine sauce in sauceboat on the side. Serve immediately. Slice at the table. Serve directly from platter to individual plates.*

PAN-FRIED FILLET OF PICKEREL
WITH A COULIS OF TOMATOES　　*Serves 4*
Filetto di Sandra con Crema di Pomodoro

4 (6-8 oz./175-250 g) fillets of fresh pickerel salt *(to taste)* freshly ground black pepper *(to taste)* juice of 1/2 lemon 1/4 tsp./1 mL peeled and finely chopped garlic 1/2 tsp./2 mL finely chopped fresh basil 1/2 tsp./2 mL finely chopped fresh oregano flour *(to dust)*	*Rinse fillets of pickerel under cold running water and pat dry with paper towels. Season with salt and pepper. Sprinkle with lemon juice, garlic, basil and oregano. Dust with flour.*
1/4 cup/50 mL olive oil	*Fry pickerel in oil in a skillet for 3-4 minutes per side until golden brown, then remove from skillet, set aside and keep warm.*
2 cups/500 mL coulis of tomatoes *(see p. 17, replacing the parsley with 1 tbsp./15 mL finely chopped fresh basil)*	*Make a bed of coulis of tomatoes on a platter. Put fillets of pickerel on top of coulis of tomatoes on platter and serve immediately. Serve directly from platter to individual plates.*

PIKE
Luccio

Background: *Pike or northern pike or jackfish are freshwater fish with long bodies, large flat jaws, mouths stretching to eyes and sharp pointed teeth. Pike may reach 9 lbs./4.5 kg, but the average market size is 2-4 lbs./1-2 kg. Smaller pike are known as pickerel and, often, the names are used interchangeably. Pike are dark mottled green in colour; the sides have golden glints and the fins and tail are reddish. They are found in lakes, ponds, rivers and streams and vie with trout as the most popular freshwater fish. They are the fastest moving of all freshwater fish and they devour enormous quantities of other fish. Their firm white flesh is low in fat content. They have few bones and a sweet flavour. Pike have always been greatly esteemed. They are available fresh, whole or in fillets, all year round.*

QUENELLES OF PIKE IN WHITE WINE-SORREL SAUCE
Polopette di Luccio al Vino Bianco

Serves 4

1 1/2 lbs./700 g fillet of fresh pike, bones removed

Rinse fillet of pike under cold running water and pat dry with paper towels. Put in a blender or food processor and process until a coarse paste is formed.

3 large eggs
4 tbsp./60 mL whipping cream
2 tbsp./30 mL brandy
zest of 1/4 lemon
dash of Worcestershire sauce
1 tsp./15 mL finely chopped fresh tarragon
1/8 tsp./pinch of ground nutmeg
1/8 tsp./pinch of mace
salt *(to taste)*
white pepper *(to taste)*

Add eggs, cream, brandy, lemon zest, Worcestershire sauce, tarragon, nutmeg, mace, salt and pepper to blender or food processor and process for 30 seconds-1 minute until mixture is well blended.

Transfer contents of blender or food processor to a bowl and chill in refrigerator for 20 minutes.

Remove bowl from refrigerator and make quenelles, or dumplings, out of fish mixture by pressing between 2 spoons or 1 spoon and wet palm of hand.

(cont'd over)

8 cups/2 L court boullion (see p. 178)

Poach quenelles in a pot of simmering court bouillon for approximately 5 minutes, then, using a slotted spoon, remove quenelles from pot and drain on paper towels. Put quenelles on a platter and set aside.

white wine-sorrel sauce (see below)

Spoon white wine-sorrel sauce over quenelles on platter and serve immediately. Serve directly from platter to individual plates.

White Wine-Sorrel Sauce:

1 cup/250 mL white wine sauce (see p. 12)

Put white wine sauce in a skillet and heat.

12-15 medium size leaves of fresh sorrel, washed and julienned

Add sorrel to skillet and simmer for 1-2 minutes.

TROUT
Trota

Background: *Trout are hard to define because there are so many species. There are river trout, lake trout and sea trout, the first two of which are best-known in North America. River trout are variously known as: brook trout, mountain trout, rainbow trout, speckled trout, Dolly Vardens and brown trout. They live in running water and have firmly-textured flesh that has a delicate flavour, except for brown trout which are more variable in flavour. They are low in fat content. Lake trout are known as: Great Lakes trout, grey trout, salmon trout, Great Lakes char and mackinaw. They range in colour from near black to light green and their flesh varies from pale ivory to deep pink, depending on their diet. They are more oily than river trout. Perhaps the best-known species among trout is the cultivated rainbow trout and its sea-going cousin, the steelhead. Rainbow trout are olive green, fading to silver through a rainbow hue on their lateral sides, and they have speckled black dots. They range in weight from 8-16 oz./250-500 g and are high in fat content. Their flesh is whiter and milder than wild trout. They are available fresh, and live, in tanks, and boned, all year round.*

BAKED FILLET OF TROUT WITH PAPAYA AND LIME
Trota al Modo Mio

Serves 4

4 (8-10 oz./250-300 g) whole fresh trout, filleted — each in 2 halves, with the head, tail and fins off
salt *(to taste)*
white pepper *(to taste)*

Rinse fillets of trout under cold running water and pat dry with paper towels. Season with salt and pepper and put fillets, skin side down, in a buttered rimmed baking tray.

1 papaya, peeled, seeded and sliced

Angle slices of papaya across fillets of trout.

juice of 1 lime

Sprinkle papaya with lime juice.

1/4 cup/50 mL dry white vermouth
4 tsp./20 mL butter

Pour vermouth over fillets in baking tray and dab each fillet with 1 tsp./ 5 mL butter.

Pre-heat oven to 375°F/190°C.

Put baking tray in oven and bake for approximately 6 minutes.

Remove baking tray from oven and put fillets of trout on a platter. Set platter aside and keep warm. Reserve liquid in tray and transfer to a saucepan. Bring to a boil, then reduce heat.

(cont'd over)

4 tbsp./60 mL butter	*Add butter to saucepan and blend in.*
juice of 1 lime	*Add lime juice to saucepan and blend in.*
zest of 1 lime	*Add lime zest to saucepan and stir in.*
1 lime, cut into 8 thin wedges	*Spoon contents of saucepan over fillets of trout on platter. Garnish platter with lime wedges and serve immediately. Serve directly from platter to individual plates.*

BAKED WHOLE TROUT STUFFED WITH MUSHROOMS
Trotelle ai Funghi

Serves 4

4 (8-10 oz./250-300 g) whole fresh trout, cleaned and boned	*Rinse trout under cold running water and pat dry with paper towels. Set aside.*
2 cups/500 mL cleaned and thinly sliced fresh mushrooms 2 tbsp./30 mL butter	*Sauté mushrooms in butter in a skillet for approximately 2 minutes.*
2 tbsp./30 mL dry white wine juice of 1 lemon 1 tbsp./15 mL peeled and finely chopped shallots 1 tbsp./15 mL finely chopped fresh parsley 1 tbsp./15 mL fresh thyme salt *(to taste)* white pepper *(to taste)*	*Add white wine, lemon juice, shallots, parsley, thyme, salt and pepper to skillet and simmer for approximately 3 minutes.*
1/4 cup/50 mL whipping cream	*Add cream to skillet and simmer for approximately 5 minutes until liquid in skillet has reduced by one-half. Set skillet aside.*
8 large leaves of radicchio, washed and dried	*Blanch leaves of radicchio in a pot of boiling water for 1 minute until they wilt, then plunge into a pot of cold water to stop the cooking. Drain pot and put radicchio leaves on paper towels to dry.*

Pre-heat oven to 350°F/180°C.

4 tsp./20 mL butter

Stuff each trout with mushroom mixture and dab with 1 tsp./5 mL butter.

Wrap centre of each trout with 2 radicchio leaves and put wrapped trout in a buttered baking tray.

Put baking tray in oven and bake for 15-20 minutes until fish are done.

lemon butter-thyme sauce
(see below)

Remove baking tray from oven and put trout, wrapped in radicchio leaves, on a platter. Pour lemon butter-thyme sauce over top of trout and serve immediately. Serve directly from platter to individual plates.

Lemon Butter-Thyme Sauce:

4 tbsp./60 mL butter

Melt butter in a saucepan.

2 tbsp./30 mL dry white wine
juice of 1/2 lemon

Add white wine and lemon juice to saucepan and blend in.

1 1/2 tsp./7 mL fresh thyme

Add thyme to saucepan and stir in. Simmer for 1-2 minutes.

BAKED WHOLE TROUT STUFFED WITH ORANGE AND TARRAGON
Trota con Arancia e Dragoncello

Serves 4

4 (8-10 oz./250-300 g) whole fresh trout, cleaned and boned
salt *(to taste)*
white pepper *(to taste)*
juice of 1 lemon
4 slices of orange
4 large sprigs of fresh tarragon
flour *(to dust)*

Rinse trout under cold running water and pat dry with paper towels. Season with salt and pepper. Sprinkle with lemon juice. Stuff each trout with 1 slice of orange and lay 1 sprig of tarragon across each orange slice. Close trout and dust with flour.

6 tbsp./90 mL olive oil
3 tbsp./45 mL butter

Sauté trout in oil and butter in a skillet for 2-3 minutes per side, then remove from skillet and put on a buttered baking tray.

Pre-heat oven to 350°F/180°C.

juice of 1 orange

Sprinkle orange juice over trout on baking tray.

Put baking tray in oven and bake for approximately 8 minutes until fish are done.

Remove baking tray from oven and put trout on a platter. Set platter aside and keep warm.

4 tbsp./60 mL butter

Melt butter in a skillet.

juice of 1 orange
juice of 1/2 lemon
3 tbsp./45 mL dry white wine

Add orange juice, lemon juice and white wine to skillet and blend in.

1 tbsp./15 mL finely chopped fresh tarragon
1 tsp./5 mL finely chopped fresh parsley

Add tarragon and parsley to skillet and stir in.

8 sections of orange, skinned, peeled and seeded

Add sections of orange to skillet and heat to warm.

Spoon contents of skillet over trout on platter — 2 sections of orange per trout — and serve immediately. Serve directly from platter to individual plates.

PAN-FRIED FILLET OF TROUT
WITH SHRIMP
Serves 4
Trotelle alla Mugnaia con Gamberetti

4 (8-10 oz./250-300 g) whole fresh trout, filleted — each in 2 halves, with the head, tail and fins off
salt *(to taste)*
white pepper *(to taste)*
juice of 1 lemon
dash of Worcestershire sauce
flour *(to dust)*

Rinse fillets of trout under cold running water and pat dry with paper towels. Season with salt and pepper. Sprinkle with lemon juice and Worcestershire sauce. Dust with flour.

6 tbsp./90 mL olive oil
3 tbsp./45 mL butter

Fry trout in oil and butter in a skillet for 1-2 minutes per side, then remove from skillet and put, skin side down, on a platter. Set platter aside and keep warm. Drain oil from skillet.

1/4 lb./125 g fresh shrimp
4 tbsp./60 mL butter

Sauté shrimp in butter in skillet for approximately 1 minute.

juice of 1 1/2 lemons

Add lemon juice to skillet and blend in.

1 1/2 tbsp./20 mL finely chopped fresh parsley

Sprinkle with parsley.

salt *(to taste)*
white pepper *(to taste)*

Season with salt and pepper.

Spoon contents of skillet over fillets of trout on platter and serve immediately. Serve directly from platter to individual plates.

POACHED WHOLE TROUT
SERVED ON A BED OF CORN WITH BUTTER, WHITE WINE AND CAPER SAUCE
Trota con Granoturco

Serves 4

4 (8-10 oz./250-300 g) whole fresh trout	*Rinse trout under cold running water and set aside.*
8 cups/2 L court bouillon *(see p. 178)*	*Put court bouillon in a pot and bring to a boil, then reduce heat to a simmer.*
	Add trout to pot and poach for 5-6 minutes, then drain pot, straining and reserving 2 tbsp./30 mL court bouillon. Set trout aside and keep warm.
3-4 cobbs of fresh corn, parboiled — to yield 1 1/2-2 cups/375-500 mL corn niblets	*Remove niblets from cobbs of corn and put in a skillet.*
1/2 cup/125 mL dry white wine 2 tbsp./30 mL court bouillon *(reserved above)*	*Add white wine and court bouillon to skillet and sauté corn niblets for 1-2 minutes.*
4 tbsp./60 mL butter	*Add butter to skillet and blend in.*
2 tbsp./30 mL drained capers	*Add capers to skillet and stir in.*
salt *(to taste)* white pepper *(to taste)*	*Season with salt and pepper.*
2 tbsp./30 mL finely chopped fresh parsley	*Transfer contents of skillet to a platter. Sprinkle with parsley. Put trout on top of corn on platter and serve immediately. Serve directly from platter to individual plates.*

WHITEFISH
Coregone

Background: *Whitefish are one of the most popular freshwater fish. Because Canada has such a large area of freshwater lakes, it has the largest catch of whitefish in the world. Whitefish are taken from deep waters of the larger lakes in the summer and through ice in the winter. They are a member of the salmon and trout family and range in weight from 1-4 lbs./500 g-2 kg, with an average weight of 2 lbs./1 kg. Whitefish are available all year round and come fresh and frozen, whole or in fillets. They have a firm, white flesh, with a delicate, almost sweet flavour. They are medium in fat content.*

PAN-FRIED FILLET OF WHITEFISH WITH TARRAGON SAUCE
Serves 4
Filetto di Coregone Salsa di Dragoncello

4 (6-8 oz./175-250 g) fillets of fresh whitefish salt *(to taste)* white pepper *(to taste)* flour *(to dust)*	*Rinse fillets of whitefish under cold running water and pat dry with paper towels. Season with salt and pepper. Dust with flour.*
3 tbsp./45 mL olive oil 1 tbsp./15 mL butter	*Fry whitefish in oil and butter in a skillet for 4-6 minutes per side until golden brown, then remove from skillet, put on a platter, set aside and keep warm. Drain oil from skillet.*
2 tbsp./30 mL dry white wine 1 tsp./5 mL tarragon vinegar 1 tbsp./15 mL peeled and finely chopped shallots 2 tsp./10 mL finely chopped fresh tarragon	*Add white wine, tarragon vinegar, shallots and tarragon to skillet and simmer for approximately 1 minute.*
1/4 cup/50 mL whipping cream	*Add cream to skillet and blend in. Simmer for approximately 3 minutes.*
1 tbsp./15 mL butter	*Add butter to skillet and blend in.*
salt *(to taste)* white pepper *(to taste)*	*Season with salt and pepper.*
	Spoon contents of skillet over fillets of whitefish on platter and serve immediately. Serve directly from platter to individual plates.

POACHED FILLET OF WHITEFISH WRAPPED WITH SLICES OF ZUCCHINI
Involtini di Coregone con Zucchini

Serves 4

4 (6 oz./175 g) fillets of fresh whitefish
salt *(to taste)*
white pepper *(to taste)*
juice of 1/2 lemon
1/4 tsp./1 mL peeled and finely chopped garlic
2 tbsp./30 mL finely chopped fresh basil
1/2 tsp./2 mL finely chopped fresh oregano
4 tbsp./60 mL extra virgin olive oil

Rinse fillets of whitefish under cold running water and pat dry with paper towels. Season with salt and pepper. Sprinkle with lemon juice, garlic, basil and oregano. Drizzle with 1 tbsp./ 15 mL olive oil per fillet.

2 medium zucchini, thinly sliced lengthwise

Wrap fillets of whitefish with slices of zucchini and secure with toothpicks.

4 tbsp./60 mL extra virgin olive oil

Put wrapped fillets in a buttered baking dish and drizzle with olive oil. Set baking dish aside.

Pre-heat oven to 375°F/190°C.

1/4 cup/50 mL fish stock *(see p. 8)*
2 tbsp./30 mL white vinegar

Put fish stock and vinegar in a saucepan and bring to a boil.

Pour contents of saucepan over fillets of whitefish in baking dish.

buttered paper

Cover baking dish with a sheet of buttered paper. Put baking dish in oven and poach for 12-14 minutes until fish is done.

Remove baking dish from oven and carefully remove wrapped fillets of whitefish from dish. Put fillets on a platter, set aside and keep warm. Reserve liquid in baking dish and transfer to a saucepan.

1/4 tsp./1 mL Dijon mustard

Add mustard to saucepan and blend in.

1 tsp./5 mL finely chopped fresh parsley

Add parsley to saucepan and stir in.

Bring contents of saucepan to a boil, then remove saucepan from heat.

3 tbsp./45 mL extra virgin olive oil	*Using a whisk, slowly add olive oil to saucepan and blend in.*
salt *(to taste)* white pepper *(to taste)*	*Season with salt and pepper.*
	Spoon contents of saucepan over wrapped fillets of whitefish on platter and serve immediately. Serve directly from platter to individual plates.

SAUTEED CUBED SCALLOP OF WHITEFISH WITH A JULIENNE OF RADICCHIO
Fette di Coregone con Radicchio

Serves 4

1 1/2 lbs./700 g fillet of fresh whitefish, cut into 2 inch/5 cm scallops, then cubed into 2 inch/ 5 cm pieces salt *(to taste)* white pepper *(to taste)* juice of 1/2 lemon flour *(to dust)*	*Rinse cubes of whitefish under cold running water and pat dry with paper towels. Season with salt and pepper. Sprinkle with lemon juice. Dust with flour.*
3 tbsp./45 mL vegetable oil 1 tbsp./15 mL olive oil	*Sauté whitefish in oil in a skillet for 3-5 minutes until golden brown. Leave whitefish in skillet.*
1 medium head of radicchio, washed, dried and julienned	*Add radicchio to skillet. Toss and heat for 1-2 minutes, then drain oil from skillet.*
3 tbsp./45 mL extra virgin olive oil 1 tbsp./15 mL balsamic vinegar	*Add extra virgin olive oil and balsamic vinegar to skillet. Toss and heat for 1-2 minutes.*
1 tsp./5 mL freshly squeezed lemon juice	*Sprinkle contents of skillet with lemon juice.*
salt *(to taste)* white pepper *(to taste)*	*Season with salt and pepper.*
	Transfer contents of skillet to a platter or individual plates and serve immediately.

CLAMS
Vongole

Background: *Clams are available on both Pacific and Atlantic coasts and come in hard-shelled and soft-shelled varieties. Hard-shelled clams dominate the Pacific coast. There are three distinct species: butter, littleneck and Manila clams. Butter clams can reach a size of 6 inches/12 cm across. They have oval-shaped shells that are generally white in colour. They are found along the West Coast in the lower third of the tidal zone, where they are harvested by digging with forks. Littleneck clams range in size up to 3 inches/6 cm across. They are oval in shape and vary in colour from white to brown. They live along the coast, slightly higher on the beach than butter clams, and are harvested with rakes. Manila clams were accidently imported from Japan in the 1930s, when oysters were imported to be cultivated. They are similar to littleneck clams in shape, but they are more elongated. They vary in colour from white to yellow to brown and are harvested with rakes along the coast at mid-to-high tide levels. Butter clams are available from November to May and are usually canned. Littleneck and Manila clams — the steamer clams — are available fresh all year round. The major species of clams on the Atlantic coast is the soft-shelled steamer clam. Soft-shelled steamer clams have an average size of 2 1/2 inches/ 5 cm across and they have brittle, elongated shells that are chalky white. The Atlantic coast also has hard-shelled littleneck clams, also known as cherrystone clams, a different species than the Pacific littleneck clam; and a larger hard-shelled clam called the quahag or quahog. The quahag or quahog have thick, greyish-white shells and they range in size up to 6 inches/12 cm across. Littleneck or cherrystone clams have thick, greyish-white shells as well, but they range in size from 2 1/2-3 1/2 inches/5-7 cm across. Atlantic soft-shelled steamer clams are harvested in controlled zones, but the smaller hard-shelled clams, the littleneck or cherrystone clams, can be found along the shoreline at low tide. All clams are low in fat content and they are less susceptible than mussels to toxic poisoning. Clams must be cleaned before using. Use a brush or plastic scrubbing pad. Because clams are salty to begin with, do not add salt when cooking with them, unless you are adding it to the ingredients that accompany the clams.*

BAKED CLAMS AND RICE WITH SAFFRON *Serves 4*
Vongole Mediterranio

2 lbs./1 kg fresh clams, washed and cleaned
1/4 cup/50 mL dry white wine
1/2 tsp./2 mL peeled and finely chopped garlic

Put clams in a pot with white wine and garlic. Cover pot and steam clams for 5-6 minutes until they open. Discard any clams that do not open. Drain pot, reserving the liquid, and remove clams from shells, leaving some clams in the shell for garnish. Set clams aside. Strain\clam liquid through a sieve lined with a linen or muslin cloth into a bowl. Set clam liquid aside.

Pre-heat oven to 300°F/150°C.

1/2 medium onion, peeled and finely chopped
3 tbsp./45 mL butter

Sauté onion in butter in an ovenproof casserole dish for 2-3 minutes until soft and transparent.

2 cups/500 mL long grain white rice
1/2 tsp./2 mL saffron threads

Add rice and saffron to casserole dish and gently stir to coat with butter.

3 cups/750 mL chicken stock *(see p. 7)* or cold water

Add chicken stock or water to casserole dish.

clam liquid *(reserved above)*

Add clam liquid to casserole dish and bring to a boil. Stir rice once, reduce heat and cover dish.

Put casserole dish in oven and bake for approximately 15 minutes.

2 tbsp./30 mL butter

Remove casserole dish from oven and uncover. Add clams and butter to dish and gently mix together.

Re-cover casserole dish. Return dish to oven and bake for an additional 5-7 minutes.

2 tbsp./30 mL washed and chopped scallions
clams in the shell *(reserved above)*

Remove casserole dish from oven and uncover. Sprinkle with scallions. Garnish with reserved clams in the shell and serve immediately. Serve directly from casserole dish to individual plates.

CLAM AND MUSSEL STEW
Cozze Adriatica

Serves 4

1 1/2 lbs./700 g fresh clams, washed and cleaned
1 lb./500 g fresh mussels, washed and cleaned

Set clams and mussels aside.

1/2 medium onion, peeled and finely chopped
3 tbsp./45 mL olive oil

Sauté onion in oil in a pot for 2-3 minutes until soft and transparent.

1/2 (14 oz./398 mL) can of chopped peeled Italian plum tomatoes —and all of the tomato liquid
1/2 tsp./2 mL peeled and finely chopped garlic
1/4 cup/50 mL dry white wine
1 sprig of fresh oregano
1 sprig of fresh rosemary
1 sprig of fresh thyme

Add tomatoes and tomato liquid, garlic, white wine, oregano, rosemary and thyme to pot and bring to a boil.

Add clams and mussels to pot. Cover pot and steam clams and mussels for 5-6 minutes until they open. Discard any clams or mussels that do not open.

freshly ground black pepper *(to taste)*

Season with pepper.

1 1/2 tsp./7 mL finely chopped fresh parsley
2 tbsp./30 mL extra virgin olive oil

Transfer contents of pot to a serving bowl. Sprinkle with parsley and drizzle with olive oil. Serve immediately. Serve directly from serving bowl to individual bowls.

STEAMED CLAMS IN WHITE WINE
Zuppa di Vongole

Serves 4

6 lbs./3 kg fresh clams, washed and cleaned

Set clams aside.

3 tbsp./45 mL peeled and finely chopped onion
2 tbsp./30 mL olive oil

Sauté onion in oil in a pot for 1-2 minutes until soft and transparent.

1/2 tsp./2 mL peeled and finely chopped garlic

Add garlic to pot and sauté for approximately 1 minute.

2/3 cup/150 mL dry white wine

Add white wine to pot and bring to a boil.

Add clams to pot. Cover pot and steam clams for 5-6 minutes until they open. Discard any clams that do not open.

3 tbsp./45 mL butter
2 tbsp./30 mL finely chopped fresh parsley

Add butter and parsley to pot and mix together.

freshly ground black pepper *(to taste)*

Season with pepper.

Transfer contents of pot to a serving bowl and serve immediately. Serve directly from serving bowl to individual bowls.

STEAMED CLAMS IN WHITE WINE WITH TOMATOES, SUNDRIED TOMATOES, ONION AND GARLIC
Vongole al Pomodoro

Serves 4

6 lbs./3 kg fresh clams, washed and cleaned

Set clams aside.

3 tbsp./45 mL peeled and finely chopped onion
2 tbsp./30 mL olive oil

Sauté onion in oil in a pot for 1-2 minutes until soft and transparent.

1 tsp./5 mL peeled and finely chopped garlic

Add garlic to pot and sauté for approximately 1 minute.

2/3 cup/150 mL dry white wine
3 tbsp./45 mL marinated sundried tomatoes, drained and chopped

Add white wine and sundried tomatoes to pot and bring to a boil.

Add clams to pot. Cover pot and steam clams for 5-6 minutes until they open. Discard any clams that do not open.

5-6 medium firm, ripe tomatoes, eyes removed and scored ''x'' on top

While clams are steaming, blanch tomatoes in a pot of rapidly boiling water for 20 seconds, then plunge into a pot of cold water to stop the cooking. Peel, seed and julienne tomatoes.

Add julienned tomatoes to pot and heat for approximately 1 minute.

2 tbsp./30 mL extra virgin olive oil
2 tbsp./30 mL finely chopped fresh parsley

Add olive oil and parsley to pot and mix together.

(cont'd over)

| salt *(to taste)*
freshly ground black pepper *(to taste)* | Season with salt and pepper. |
| | Transfer contents of pot to a serving bowl and serve immediately. Serve directly from serving bowl to individual bowls. |

STEAMED CLAMS
WITH MARINARA SAUCE
Vongole alla Marinara

Serves 4

6 lbs./3 kg fresh clams, washed and cleaned	Set clams aside.
2 tbsp./30 mL peeled and finely chopped onion 2 tbsp./30 mL olive oil	Sauté onion in oil in a pot for 1-2 minutes until soft and transparent.
1/2 tsp./2 mL peeled and finely chopped garlic 1 tsp./5 mL washed and finely chopped fillet of anchovy	Add garlic and anchovies to pot and sauté for approximately 1 minute.
4 cups/1 L tomato sauce *(see p. 11)*	Add tomato sauce to pot and bring to a boil.
	Add clams to pot. Cover pot and steam clams for 5-6 minutes until they open. Discard any clams that do not open.
salt *(to taste)* freshly ground black pepper *(to taste)*	Season with salt and pepper.
1 tbsp./15 mL finely chopped fresh parsley	Transfer contents of pot to a serving bowl. Sprinkle with parsley and serve immediately. Serve directly from serving bowl to individual bowls.

STEAMED CLAMS WITH PROSCIUTTO
Vongole Contadina

Serves 4

6 lbs./3 kg fresh clams, washed and cleaned

Set clams aside.

2-3 oz./50-75 g prosciutto, julienned
1 whole clove of garlic, peeled
2 tbsp./30 mL olive oil
2 tbsp./30 mL butter

Sauté prosciutto and garlic in oil and butter in a pot for approximately 1 minute.

1/4 cup/50 mL dry white wine
1/2 cup/125 mL whipping cream

Add white wine to pot, then, 30 seconds later, add cream to pot and bring to a boil.

Add clams to pot. Cover pot and steam clams for 5-6 minutes until they open. Discard any clams that do not open.

2 tbsp./30 mL butter
2 tbsp./30 mL finely chopped flat-leaved Italian parsley

Add butter and parsley to pot and mix together.

freshly ground black pepper *(to taste)*

Season with pepper.

Transfer contents of pot to a serving bowl and serve immediately. Serve directly from serving bowl to individual bowls.

CRAB
Granchio

Background: *Crab are available in both Pacific and Atlantic oceans. The most popular species on the Pacific coast is the Dungeness crab, also known as the market crab or common crab. They weigh between 1 1/2-3 1/2 lbs./700 g-1.75 kg and are caught in traps. They are available fresh from May through October and are sold whole, live or cooked, and as fresh or frozen meat. Dungeness crab are reddish brown to purple on top and cream to yellow underneath when they are fresh and they turn bright orange to red when cooked. Another popular species on the West Coast, sought after for its legs, is the Alaska king crab. On the Atlantic coast, the snow crab, sometimes called the spider or queen crab, is the most popular species. Snow crab have an average weight of 2 1/2 lbs./1.25 kg and are caught from June through October. They are generally available as frozen claws and legs, or in bulk form as fresh or frozen meat. Also available, but not natural to Canada, is the soft-shell or blue crab, which weighs approximately 3-4 oz./75-125 g without their hard shells. Their habitat is the south Atlantic ocean and the coast of the Gulf of Mexico. These crab are harvested as they shed their hard outer shell and they are eaten whole. All crab are low in fat content. After shrimp, they are the most popular shellfish.*

CRAB AND MUSHROOMS
IN A PUFF PASTRY
Sfogliatelle di Granchio

Serves 4

1/2 lb./250 g fresh crabmeat	*Put crabmeat in a bowl and set aside.*
1/2 cup/125 mL cleaned and sliced fresh mushrooms 1 tbsp./15 mL peeled and finely chopped shallots 2 tbsp./30 mL butter	*Sauté mushrooms and shallots in butter in a skillet for approximately 2 minutes.*
1 tbsp./15 mL dry white wine 1 tbsp./15 mL freshly squeezed lemon juice	*Add white wine and lemon juice to skillet and simmer for approximately 3 minutes.*
1/4 cup/50 mL whipping cream	*Add cream to skillet, blend in and bring to a boil. Reduce heat and simmer for approximately 2 minutes.*
3/4 cup/175 mL Béchamel sauce *(see p. 8)* or white wine sauce *(see p. 12)*	*Add Béchamel sauce or white wine sauce to skillet, blend in and bring to a boil. Reduce heat and simmer for approximately 2 minutes.*
	Add crabmeat to skillet and stir in. Do not heat.
1/2 tsp./2 mL fresh thyme	*Season with thyme.*
	Pre-heat oven to 375°F/190°C.
prepared puff pastry	*Roll out pastry until it is 1/8 inch/ 3 mm thin and cut into 8 (4 x 4 inch/ 10 x 10 cm) squares.*
	Spoon one-eighth of the crab mixture into the centre of each pastry square.
1 egg, beaten	*Brush 2 edges of each pastry square with egg and fold into triangle shapes. Press edges with a fork to seal and brush triangles with remaining egg.*
1/4-1/2 cup/50-125 mL lemon butter *(see p. 95)* tomato and lettuce salad *(to accompany)*	*Put triangles on a buttered baking tray. Put baking tray in oven and bake for 10-12 minutes until golden. Remove tray from oven and put triangles on a platter. Serve immediately. Serve directly from platter to individual plates — 2 triangles per plate. Serve with lemon butter in a sauceboat on the side. Serve with a tomato and lettuce salad.*

CRAB PIE
Torta di Granchio

Serves 4-6

1 (9 inch/23 cm) pre-baked pie shell *(or see recipe for pie crust, p. 19, and pre-bake)*

Set pie shell aside.

1 lb./500 g fresh crabmeat
3 tbsp./45 mL washed and chopped scallions
2 tbsp./30 mL dry white vermouth
juice of 1/2 lemon
zest of 1/4 lemon
1 tsp./5 mL finely chopped fresh parsley
1 tsp./5 mL fresh thyme
freshly ground black pepper *(to taste)*

Put crabmeat, scallions, vermouth, lemon juice, lemon zest, parsley, thyme and pepper in a bowl and gently mix together.

Evenly spread crab mixture over bottom of pie shell.

3 eggs
1 1/2 cups/375 mL whipping cream

Mix eggs and cream together in a bowl.

1/8 tsp./pinch of salt
1/8 tsp./pinch of white pepper
1/8 tsp./pinch of ground nutmeg

Season with salt, pepper and nutmeg.

Pour egg mixture over crab mixture in pie shell. Pour only to the depth of the edge of the pie shell. Do not flood shell.

1 firm, ripe tomato, eye removed — cut into 6 slices

Put slices of tomato on top of egg mixture.

freshly ground black pepper *(to taste)*
1/2 cup/125 mL freshly grated Mozzarella cheese
3 tbsp./45 mL freshly grated Parmesan cheese

Sprinkle tomato with pepper, then sprinkle with Mozzarella and Parmesan cheeses.

Pre-heat oven to 325°F/160°C.

Put pie shell on a baking tray. Put baking tray in oven and bake for 35-45 minutes until centre of pie is firm to the touch.

green salad *(to accompany)*

Remove tray from oven and allow pie to set and cool for 10 minutes. Cut into wedges at the table and serve on individual plates. Serve with a large crisp green salad.

GRATINEED CRAB AND SCALLOPS
Granchio Veneziano

Serves 4

1 lb./500 g fresh crabmeat	*Put crabmeat in a bowl and set aside.*
1/2 lb./250 g fresh scallops 4 tbsp./60 mL butter	*Sauté scallops in butter in a skillet for approximately 1 minute, then, using a slotted spoon, remove from skillet and put in a bowl. Set aside and keep warm.*
1 tbsp./15 mL peeled and finely chopped shallots	*Add shallots to skillet and sauté for approximately 1 minute.*
1/4 cup/50 mL dry white wine juice of 1 lemon	*Add white wine and lemon juice to skillet and simmer for 1-2 minutes.*
1/2 cup/125 mL whipping cream	*Add cream to skillet, blend in and simmer for 2-3 minutes.*
1 1/2 cups/375 mL Béchamel sauce (see p. 8)	*Add Béchamel sauce to skillet, blend in and bring to a boil. Reduce heat and simmer for approximately 2 minutes.*
	Add crabmeat and scallops to skillet, stir and heat.
2 tbsp./30 mL chopped fresh chives	*Add chives to skillet and stir in.*
salt *(to taste)* white pepper *(to taste)*	*Season with salt and pepper.*
	Pre-heat oven to broil/grill.
	Put crab and scallop mixture in clean, dry crab shells or on large clean, dry scallop shells.
4 tbsp./60 mL fresh fine white breadcrumbs 2 tbsp./30 mL freshly grated Parmesan cheese	*Sprinkle with breadcrumbs and Parmesan cheese.*
	Put crab or scallop shells on a baking tray. Put baking tray in oven and broil/grill for 2-4 minutes until golden brown.
	Remove tray from oven and transfer shells to individual plates. Serve immediately.

WHOLE DUNGENESS CRAB STUFFED
WITH SPINACH AND MUSHROOMS
Granchio con Spinaci e Funghi

Serves 4

4 (1 1/2 lb./700 g) whole fresh
Dungeness crab — plus 3/4 lb./350 g
fresh crabmeat
24 cups/6 L cold water
1/4 cup/50 mL salt

Cook crab in a pot of rapidly boiling salted water for 12-14 minutes, then remove crab from pot and cool under cold running water just enough to be able to handle. Pull off top shell, leaving claws and legs intact and attached to body. Leave meat in claws, legs and body and set aside. Thoroughly rinse crab body, however, and shell, of entrails. Dry shell and set aside. Put the 3/4 lb./350 g crabmeat in a bowl and set aside.

6-8 bunches of fresh spinach
washed and stemmed
2 tbsp./30 mL dry white wine
1/4 tsp./1 mL peeled and
finely chopped garlic
salt *(to taste)*
white pepper *(to taste)*

Cook spinach in a pot containing white wine, garlic, salt and pepper for approximately 1 minute until spinach has just wilted, then drain pot and coarsely chop spinach. Put spinach in a bowl and set aside.

2 cups/500 mL cleaned and
finely chopped fresh mushrooms
2 tbsp./30 mL peeled and
finely chopped shallots
1/2 tsp./2 mL peeled and
finely chopped garlic
4 tbsp./60 mL butter

Sauté mushrooms, shallots and garlic in butter in a skillet for 3-4 minutes, then add to spinach in bowl and gently mix together. Set aside.

2 tbsp./30 mL dry white wine
or vermouth
juice of 1 lemon

Put white wine or vermouth and lemon juice in a skillet and heat.

1/4 cup/50 mL whipping cream

Add cream to skillet and blend in.

1 1/2 cups/375 mL Béchamel sauce
(see p. 8)

Add Béchamel sauce to skillet, blend in and bring to a boil. Reduce heat and simmer for approximately 2 minutes.

Add crabmeat in bowl and spinach-mushroom mixture in skillet to skillet with Béchamel sauce. Gently mix together and heat.

salt *(to taste)*
white pepper *(to taste)*
1/8 tsp./pinch of ground nutmeg

Season with salt, pepper and nutmeg.

Pre-heat oven to 375°F/190°C.

Spoon crabmeat-spinach-mushroom mixture into crab shells.

4 tbsp./60 mL freshly grated Parmesan cheese

Sprinkle with Parmesan cheese.

Put crab shells on a baking tray. Put baking tray in oven and bake for 10-12 minutes.

While crabmeat mixture in shell is baking, return crab claws, legs and body to pot of rapidly boiling salted water for 2-3 minutes to heat, then drain just before crabmeat mixture is done.

1 tbsp./15 mL finely chopped fresh parsley
8 strips of drained sliced pimento
4 scallions, washed and trimmed at both ends to fit shell
— white ends dipped in paprika
lemon butter *(see below)*
(to accompany)

Arrange crab claws, legs and body on individual plates. Remove baking tray from oven and cradle crab shells, with crabmeat mixture, in the middle of crab claws and legs — in front of crab body. Sprinkle crabmeat mixture with parsley and lay 2 strips of sliced pimento across crabmeat mixture in a cross formation. Lay trimmed and dipped scallions across pimentos, white part facing forward, and serve immediately. Serve with lemon butter in bowls on the side. Serve with a nutcracker and picks.

Lemon Butter:

1 tbsp./15 mL peeled and finely chopped shallots
3 tbsp./45 mL dry white wine
juice of 1 lemon

Sauté shallots in white wine and lemon juice in a saucepan for 1-2 minutes.

1/2 cup/125 mL butter

Add butter to saucepan and blend in, then remove saucepan from heat.

salt *(to taste)*
white pepper *(to taste)*

Season with salt and pepper.

Transfer contents of saucepan to individual bowls and serve warm.

LOBSTER
Astaco

Background: *American or northern or Maine lobster is found in the Atlantic ocean, but is shipped by container and flown by air all over the world. Lobsters are caught from March through December, but they are available fresh and live, cooked and frozen, whole or part, all year round. They are at their best from 1-2 lbs./ 500 g-1 kg. Their colour varies greatly, but they are usually orange-red to blue-green. They turn bright red when cooked. Their meat is low in fat content, but rich. Lobsters are probably the most flavourful of all crustaceans. They are the most prized of all shellfish. American lobster is not to be confused with spiny lobster, also known as rock lobster, crayfish or langouste. Spiny lobsters are found in warm coastal waters all over the world and they are readily available, fresh and frozen, all year round. They are similar to the American lobster in colouring, but with brighter mottling and no claws. They range in weight from 1-4 lbs./500 g-2 kg and are widely used, most commonly as steak and lobster. Spiny lobster meat is extremely popular as decoration, especially in buffets.*

BAKED LOBSTER
WITH MUSTARD AND OREGANO
Serves 4
Astaco Piccante Umberto

4 (1 1/2 lb./700 g) fresh lobsters
24 cups/6 L court bouillon
(see recipe, p. 178, and triple cold water)

Cook lobsters in a pot of rapidly boiling court bouillon for 10-12 minutes, then remove lobsters from pot and cool under cold running water. Using a large kitchen knife, cut lobsters in half from head to tail. Remove entrails from lobster by mouth and discard. Crack claws, using the flat side of knife, and remove meat from claws. Chop meat from claws and set aside. Remove meat from tail and slice in rounds. Put lobster meat in a bowl and set aside. Reserve shell of lobster and set aside.

salt *(to taste)*
white pepper *(to taste)*

Season lobster meat in bowl with salt and pepper.

2 eggs, beaten
1/2 cup/125 mL melted butter
4 tbsp./60 mL olive oil
4 tbsp./60 mL Dijon mustard
1 tbsp./15 mL finely chopped fresh oregano

Add eggs, butter, olive oil, mustard and oregano to lobster meat in bowl and mix together thoroughly.

Return lobster meat to lobster shells.

Pre-heat oven to 350°F/180°C.

Put lobster shells on a buttered baking tray.

Put baking tray in oven and bake for approximately 10 minutes.

2 lemons, cut into 8 wedges
4 large sprigs of fresh parsley

Remove baking tray from oven. Arrange lobster shells on a platter. Garnish platter with lemon wedges and sprigs of parsley. Serve immediately. Serve directly from platter to individual plates.

BROILED LOBSTER
WITH SHERRY-GINGER SAUCE
Astaco Brasata allo Zenzero

Serves 4

Pre-heat oven to broil/grill

4 (1 1/2 lb./700 g) fresh lobsters
salt *(to taste)*
white pepper *(to taste)*
2 tbsp./30 mL melted butter
1/2 tsp./2 mL peeled and finely chopped garlic
1 tsp./5 mL peeled and finely chopped fresh ginger root

Using a large kitchen knife, kill lobsters by cutting them in half lengthwise from head to tail. Remove entrails from lobster by mouth and discard. Crack claws using the flat side of knife. Leave meat of tail in the shell. Put lobster halves, shell side down, on a baking tray. Season with salt and pepper. Sprinkle with lime juice and brush with butter, then sprinkle with garlic and ginger.

Put baking tray in oven and broil/grill for 8-10 minutes until lobster meat is firm. Do not overcook.

sherry-ginger sauce *(see below)*

Remove baking tray from oven. Arrange lobster halves on individual plates and serve immediately. Serve with a nutcracker. Serve with sherry-ginger sauce in a sauceboat on the side.

(cont'd over)

Sherry-Ginger Sauce:

1/4 tsp./1 mL peeled and finely chopped garlic 1 tsp./5 mL peeled and finely chopped fresh ginger root 1/2 cup/125 mL dry sherry	Soak garlic and ginger in sherry in a saucepan for 2 hours.
	Bring saucepan to a boil, reduce heat and simmer for approximately 3 minutes, then remove saucepan from heat.
6 tbsp./90 mL butter	Using a whisk, add butter to saucepan and blend in.
juice of 1 lime	Add lime juice to saucepan and blend in.
salt *(to taste)* white pepper *(to taste)*	Season with salt and pepper.
	Transfer contents of saucepan to a sauceboat and serve warm.

Make the sherry-ginger sauce ahead.

GRATINEED MEDALLIONS OF LOBSTER WITH TRUFFLE SAUCE
Medaglioni d' Astaco Dorati

Serves 4

4 (1 1/4-1 1/2 lb./550-700 g) fresh lobsters	Using a large kitchen knife, kill lobsters by splitting head in half lengthwise. Cut off claws and, using the flat side of knife, crack and remove meat from claws. Chop meat into 1/2 inch/1 cm pieces and put on a buttered baking tray. Twist and pull tail away from body. Using scissors, cut the underside of tail down the centre. Remove meat from tail and slice in rounds. Put rounds of lobster on baking tray. Discard lobster carcass.

salt *(to taste)*
white pepper *(to taste)*
juice of 1 lemon
1/2 tsp./2 mL peeled and
finely chopped garlic

*Season lobster meat with salt and pepper.
Sprinkle with lemon juice and garlic
and set aside.*

Pre-heat oven to broil/grill.

2/3 cup/150 mL fresh fine white
breadcrumbs
2 tbsp./30 mL finely chopped
fresh parsley

*Put breadcrumbs and parsley in a
bowl and mix together.*

*Sprinkle breadcrumb mixture over
lobster meat on baking tray.*

4 tbsp./60 mL melted butter

Drizzle with butter.

*Put baking tray in oven and broil/grill
for 4-5 minutes until meat is firm.
Do not overcook.*

truffle sauce *(see below)*

*Remove baking tray from oven and put
lobster on a platter or individual plates.
Serve immediately. Serve with truffle
sauce in a sauceboat on the side.*

Truffle Sauce:

1 tbsp./15 mL peeled and
finely chopped shallots
1 tbsp./15 mL butter

*Sauté shallots in butter in a skillet
for approximately 1 minute.*

1/4 cup/50 mL port wine

Add port to skillet and flambé.

1 cup/250 mL white wine sauce
(see p. 12)

*When flame dies down, add white
wine sauce to skillet and blend in.
Simmer for 2-3 minutes.*

1 tsp./5 mL freshly grated truffles
— or 2 tsp./10 mL white truffle paste

*Add truffles or truffle paste to skillet
and blend in.*

*Transfer contents of skillet to a
sauceboat and serve warm.*

MUSSELS
Cozze

Background: *Mussels grow wild and they are grown commercially on both Pacific and Atlantic coasts. Mussels have long been popular in Europe and are gaining popularity in North America. In fact, there is more interest in mussels now than in any other shellfish. This is because they are extremely versatile and tasty. Mussels are blue to black molluscs. They have smooth shells and beards — bunches of fibre attached to their shells. When cultivated, their flesh is tender, plump and delicately flavoured. Mussels are available fresh all year round. They are less available in the summer when warmer waters bring a proliferation of plankton that can poison mussels. It is best to check with your fisheries department before harvesting wild mussels in the summertime, as they may be unsafe. Mussels must be cleaned just before using them. Remove their beards with a quick tug and scrub their shells with a brush or plastic cleaning pad. Use only live mussels — mussels whose shells are tightly closed; whose shells do not move when twisted.*

BAKED MUSSELS
WITH PIZZAIOLA SAUCE
Cozze al Forno Pizzaiola

Serves 4

6 lbs./3 kg fresh mussels, washed and cleaned

Set mussels aside.

2 tbsp./30 mL peeled and finely chopped onion
2 tbsp./30 mL olive oil

Sauté onion in oil in a pot for 1-2 minutes until soft and transparent.

1/4 tsp./1 mL peeled and finely chopped garlic

Add garlic to pot and sauté for approximately 1 minute.

1/2 cup/125 mL dry white wine

Add white wine to pot and bring to a boil.

Add mussels to pot. Cover pot and steam mussels for 5-6 minutes until they open. Discard any mussels that do not open. Drain pot, reserving the liquid, and put mussels, in the shell, on a baking tray. Strain mussel liquid through a sieve lined with a linen or muslin cloth into a bowl and set aside.

Pre-heat oven to 375°F/190°C.

pizzaiola sauce *(see below)* — *Spoon 1 1/2 tsp./7 mL pizzaiola sauce over each open mussel on baking tray.*

3 tbsp./45 mL freshly grated Parmesan cheese — *Sprinkle Parmesan cheese over top of pizzaiola sauce.*

Put baking tray in the oven and bake for approximately 5 minutes.

2 tbsp./30 mL finely chopped fresh parsley — *Remove baking tray from oven and put mussels on a platter or individual plates. Sprinkle with parsley and serve immediately.*

Pizzaiola Sauce: — *Makes 3-3 1/2 cups/750-875 mL*

1/2 medium onion, peeled and finely chopped 3 tbsp./45 mL olive oil — *Sauté onion in oil in a skillet for 2-3 minutes until soft and transparent.*

1/4 tsp./1 mL peeled and finely chopped garlic — *Add garlic to skillet and sauté for approximately 1 minute.*

3 fillets of anchovy, washed and chopped — *Add anchovies to skillet.*

mussel liquid *(reserved above)* — *Add mussel liquid to skillet and reduce by simmering until 1/2 cup/125 mL remains.*

3 cups/750 mL tomato sauce *(see p. 11)* — *Add tomato sauce to skillet, blend in and bring to a boil. Reduce heat and simmer for approximately 3 minutes until sauce thickens slightly. Skim sauce.*

3 tbsp./45 mL drained capers — *Add capers to skillet and stir in.*

salt *(to taste)* freshly ground black pepper *(to taste)* 1 1/2 tbsp./20 mL finely chopped fresh oregano — *Season with salt, pepper and oregano.*

Leftover pizzaiola sauce may be stored in a sealed plastic container in the refrigerator for approximately 1 week. To make this sauce fresh for other recipes, omit the mussel liquid and continue.

MUSSELS
WITH EGG AND ASPARAGUS TIPS
Cozze Strapazzate

Serves 4

4 lbs./2 kg fresh mussels, washed and cleaned	*Set mussels aside.*
2 tbsp./30 mL peeled and finely chopped onion 2 tbsp./30 mL olive oil	*Sauté onion in oil in a pot for 1-2 minutes until soft and transparent.*
1/4 tsp./1 mL peeled and finely chopped garlic	*Add garlic to pot and sauté for approximately 1 minute.*
1/2 cup/125 mL dry white wine	*Add white wine to pot and bring to a boil.*
	Add mussels to pot. Cover pot and steam mussels for 5-6 minutes until they open. Discard any mussels that do not open. Drain pot, reserving 1/2 cup/ 125 mL liquid, and remove mussels from shells. Set mussels aside and strain liquid through sieve lined with a linen or muslin cloth into a bowl. Set mussel liquid aside.
12 spears of fresh asparagus, washed, peeled and trimmed — use only the asparagus tips	*Steam asparagus tips over boiling water in a pot for 4-5 minutes until just tender and still bright green, then drain pot and set asparagus aside.*
8 eggs, beaten	*Put eggs in a bowl.*
salt *(to taste)* white pepper *(to taste)*	*Season with salt and pepper and set aside.*
1 tbsp./15 mL olive oil 2 tbsp./30 mL butter 1/2 cup/125 mL mussel liquid *(reserved above)*	*Heat mussels in oil, butter and mussel liquid for approximately 1-2 minutes.*
	Add eggs to skillet and heat.
	Arrange asparagus tips in skillet.
2 tbsp./30 mL washed and chopped scallions	*Sprinkle with scallions.*
	Cook contents of skillet for 2-3 minutes until eggs are firm, then remove skillet from heat. Cut eggs into wedges in skillet and serve from skillet to individual plates. Serve immediately.

OYSTERS
Ostriche

Background: *Oysters grow in shallow water along the edge of both the Pacific and the Atlantic ocean. They often bear the name of the place where they are bred. They vary in size and taste according to the temperature of the water and the prevailing conditions in their breeding grounds. Pacific oysters used to be imported from Japan, but, now, they are grown locally. They are generally grey in colour, with irregular-shaped, highly-fluted shells. Their shells can reach up to 15 inches/30 cm in size, but they are usually harvested at 5-6 inches/10-12 cm, when they taste better. Commercially grown oysters are available all year round. Wild oysters are best from September to April. On the Atlantic, there are Blue Point and Malpeque oysters, the latter of which are highly prized; Cape Cod Chincoteagues, Apalachicolas, Chesapeake and Kent Island oysters, commonly known as American oysters; and the Belon oyster, grown in Nova Scotia, which is commonly known as the European oyster. Atlantic oysters vary in shape, size and colour. Their shells can be flat or deep or rounded. They are harvested from natural beds and from beds in leased areas. They are available fresh, in the shell or shucked, and frozen, shucked, in the fall and winter. Oysters are low in fat content and have rich, forceful meat which has a sweet flavour. They are high in calcium and vitamin E. Throughout history, they have always been considered a delicacy.*

BAKED OYSTERS AND SPINACH SERVED WITH WALNUT SAUCE
Ostriche alla Medici

Serves 4

1 1/2 lbs./700 g fresh oysters, shucked, reserving the bottom shells — 20-24 oysters

Put oyster meat in a bowl and set aside. Put bottoms of oyster shells in a pot of rapidly boiling water for approximately 1 minute, then remove from pot, pat dry and set aside.

4-6 bunches of fresh spinach, washed and stemmed
2 tbsp./30 mL pernod
2 tbsp./30 mL peeled and finely chopped onion
1/2 tsp./2 mL peeled and finely chopped garlic
salt *(to taste)*
white pepper *(to taste)*
1/8 tsp./pinch of ground nutmeg

Cook spinach in a pot containing pernod, onion, garlic, salt, pepper and nutmeg for approximately 1 minute until spinach has just wilted, then drain pot and coarsely chop spinach.

Put approximately 1 tbsp./15 mL spinach in the centre of each oyster shell and set aside.

(cont'd over)

	Blanch oyster meat in a pot of rapidly boiling water for approximately 1 minute to firm up, then drain pot and put oyster meat on top of spinach on shells.
walnut sauce *(see below)*	*Spoon walnut sauce over oyster meat on shells to cover meat.*
	Pre-heat oven to 400°F/200°C.
	Put oyster shells on a baking tray. Put baking tray in oven and bake for 5-7 minutes.
juice of 1/2 lemon 2 tbsp./30 mL shelled and finely chopped fresh walnuts 2 tbsp./30 mL finely chopped fresh parsley	*Remove baking tray from oven and put oyster shells on individual plates, 5-6 shells per plate. Sprinkle with lemon juice, walnuts and parsley and serve immediately.*

Walnut Sauce:

1 1/2 cups/375 mL white wine sauce *(see p. 12)*	*Put white wine sauce in a saucepan and heat.*
4 tbsp./60 mL shelled and finely chopped fresh walnuts	*Add walnuts to saucepan and stir in, then remove saucepan from heat.*
2 egg yolks	*Add egg yolks to saucepan and blend in.*
1 tsp./5 mL freshly squeezed lemon juice	*Add lemon juice to saucepan and blend in.*
salt *(to taste)* white pepper *(to taste)*	*Season with salt and pepper.*

PAN-FRIED OYSTERS
Ostriche Fritte

Serves 4

1 1/2 lbs./700 g fresh oysters, shucked — 20-24 oysters
salt *(to taste)*
white pepper *(to taste)*
juice of 1 lemon
dash of Worcestershire sauce
flour *(to coat)*

Put oyster meat in a bowl and season with salt and pepper. Sprinkle with lemon juice and Worcestershire sauce. Dredge in flour.

5 eggs
4 tbsp./60 mL whipping cream
1/3 cup/75 mL freshly grated Parmesan cheese
1/4 tsp./1 mL peeled and finely chopped garlic
1/8 tsp./pinch of ground nutmeg
1/8 tsp./pinch of paprika
1/8 tsp./pinch of mace
1/8 tsp./pinch of salt

Mix eggs, cream, Parmesan cheese, garlic, nutmeg, paprika, mace and salt together in a bowl to form a batter.

Dip oyster meat in batter to coat.

1/3 cup/75 mL vegetable oil
2 tbsp./30 mL butter

Fry oysters, several at a time, in oil and butter in a skillet for 3-4 minutes per side until golden brown, then remove from skillet and drain on paper towels. Put oysters on a platter, set aside and keep warm.

1/2 cup/125 mL butter

Melt butter in a skillet.

3 tbsp./45 mL washed and chopped scallions

Add scallions to skillet, stir to coat in butter, then pour immediately over oysters on platter.

4 lemons, cut into wedges

Garnish platter with lemon wedges and serve immediately. Serve directly from platter to individual plates, 5-6 oysters per plate.

PRAWNS
Gamberoni

Background: *Prawns are large shrimp. They are sold fresh and cooked, cleaned, with the shells on or off, or in the shell. Prawns are available in all sizes and there are a great number of species, both local and imported. Although local fresh prawns are not always as large as those that are imported, they are likely to be fresher. Prawns are low in fat content and they are available, fresh and frozen, all year round.*

GRILLED SKEWERS OF PRAWNS MARINATED IN LIME JUICE AND GARLIC
Spiedino di Gamberoni

Serves 4

2 lbs./1 kg fresh prawn tails, shells left on — 32-40 prawn tails

Rinse prawns under cold running water and set aside to drain.

marinade *(see below)*

Put prawns in marinade in a baking dish in the refrigerator for 2 hours, then remove dish from refrigerator. Drain prawns and reserve marinade for basting while prawns are barbecuing.

4 wooden skewers, soaked in cold water

Thread prawns onto water-soaked wooden skewers, 8-10 prawns per skewer.

Put skewers on the oiled rack of a barbecue and cook over hot coals for 3-4 minutes per side, basting with marinade, until prawns are slightly transparent. Do not overcook.

2 limes, cut in half
2 1/2 cups/625 mL cooked long grain white rice *(to accompany)*

When prawns are done, remove skewers from barbecue and put on individual plates. Serve with lime halves. Serve immediately. Serve with rice.

Marinade:

1/2 cup/125 mL olive oil
juice of 2 limes
zest of 1 lime
1 tsp./5 mL peeled and finely chopped garlic
1 tsp./5 mL peeled and finely chopped fresh ginger root
2 tbsp./30 mL finely chopped fresh parsley
white pepper *(to taste)*

Mix olive oil, lime juice, lime zest, garlic, ginger, parsley and pepper together in a baking dish.

PAN-FRIED PRAWNS
WITH ZUCCHINI AND TOMATO SAUCE   *Serves 4*
Gamberoni Fritti con Zucchini e Pomodoro

1 1/2 lbs./700 g peeled and deveined fresh prawn tails — 20-24 prawn tails
salt *(to taste)*
freshly ground black pepper *(to taste)*
juice of 1 lemon
6 drops of Worcestershire sauce
1/8 tsp./pinch of finely chopped fresh oregano
flour *(to dust)*

Rinse prawns under cold running water and set aside to drain. Season with salt and pepper. Sprinkle with lemon juice, Worcestershire sauce and oregano. Dust with flour.

1/4 cup/50 mL olive oil
1 tbsp./15 mL butter

Fry prawns in oil and butter in a skillet for approximately 1 minute per side, then remove from skillet, put on a platter, set aside and keep warm. Reserve oil in skillet.

1 medium zucchini, washed and julienned

Add zucchini to skillet and sauté for approximately 2 minutes, then drain oil from skillet.

2 cups/500 mL tomato sauce *(see p. 11)*, puréed

Add puréed tomato sauce to skillet and bring to a boil. Reduce heat and simmer for 3-5 minutes.

2 tbsp./30 mL extra virgin olive oil

Add olive oil to skillet and blend in.

salt *(to taste)*
freshly ground black pepper *(to taste)*

Season with salt and pepper.

Return prawns to skillet. Toss and heat for 1-2 minutes.

2 tbsp./30 mL finely chopped fresh parsley

Transfer contents of skillet to a platter or individual plates. Sprinkle with parsley and serve immediately.

SAUTEED PRAWNS
IN LEMON JUICE AND GARLIC
Gamberoni alla Spagnola

Serves 4

1 1/2 lbs./700 g fresh prawn tails, shells left on
— 20-24 prawn tails
salt *(to taste)*
white pepper *(to taste)*
juice of 1/2 lemon
1/4 tsp./1 mL peeled and finely chopped garlic

Rinse prawns under cold running water and set aside to drain. Season with salt and pepper. Sprinkle with lemon juice and garlic.

1/4 cup/50 mL peanut oil

Sauté prawns in oil in a skillet for 1-2 minutes per side, then remove from skillet, put on a platter, set aside and keep warm. Drain oil from skillet.

3 tbsp./45 mL butter
3 tbsp./45 mL dry white wine
juice of 1 lemon
1/2 tsp./2 mL peeled and finely chopped garlic
2 tsp./10 mL finely chopped fresh parsley
1/8 tsp./pinch of seeded and finely chopped hot red chili pepper

Add butter, white wine, lemon juice, garlic, parsley and chili pepper to skillet and bring to a boil. Reduce heat and simmer for approximately 1 minute.

Return prawns to skillet. Toss and heat for approximately 2 minutes.

Transfer contents of skillet to a platter and serve immediately. Serve directly from platter to individual plates.

SCALLOPS
Capesante

Background: *Scallops are free-moving molluscs that live in the ocean. When one eats a scallop, one is really eating the muscle of the scallop. Scallop muscles are large because scallops are always moving on the ocean floor and always opening and closing their shells. Scallop shells are easily opened and they are usually shucked right away. Scallops are graded according to size, bay scallops being the smallest. There are over 400 species of scallops worldwide, but the sea scallop of both the Pacific and the Atlantic ocean and the bay scallop of only the Atlantic ocean are the most commonly harvested species. Sea scallop shells range in size from 5-10 inches/ 10-20 cm across. Bay scallop shells are much smaller — about 2 inches/4 cm across. Scallops are low in fat content and have a unique, rich flavour. They are available fresh all year round, but are more readily available in the summer. Bay scallops are not available all year round because their catch is regulated locally.*

PAN-FRIED SCALLOPS ITALIAN STYLE   *Serves 4*
Bigne Capesante

1 1/2 lbs./700 g fresh scallops
salt *(to taste)*
freshly ground black pepper *(to taste)*
juice of 1 lemon
1/4-1/2 tsp./1-2 mL peeled and finely chopped garlic
flour *(to dust)*

Rinse scallops under cold running water and set aside to drain. Season with salt and pepper. Sprinkle with lemon juice, garlic and oregano. Dust with flour.

1/3 cup/75 mL olive oil

Fry scallops in oil in a skillet for 3-4 minutes per side until slightly brown, then remove from skillet, put on a platter, set aside and keep warm.

1 (14 oz./398 mL) can of peeled Italian plum tomatoes, drained and chopped
2 tbsp./30 mL marinated sundried tomatoes, drained and chopped
2 tbsp./30 mL drained capers
2 tbsp./30 mL dry white wine
2 tbsp./30 mL finely chopped fresh basil

Add tomatoes, sundried tomatoes, capers, white wine and oregano to skillet and bring to a boil. Reduce and simmer for 3-5 minutes.

salt *(to taste)*
freshly ground black pepper *(to taste)*

Season with salt and pepper.

(cont'd over)

2 tbsp./30 mL extra virgin olive oil

Return scallops to skillet and heat for approximately 2 minutes.

Add olive oil to skillet and blend in.

1 lb./500 g egg or spinach fettuccine, cooked and buttered *(to accompany)*

Make a bed of fettuccine on individual plates. Spoon contents of skillet over fettuccine on plates and serve immediately.

PAN-FRIED SCALLOPS SERVED WITH HORSERADISH BUTTER
Capesante con Burro di Rapa

Serves 4

1 1/2 lbs./700 g fresh scallops
salt *(to taste)*
white pepper *(to taste)*
juice of 1 lemon
flour *(to dust)*

Rinse scallops under cold running water and set aside to drain. Season with salt and pepper. Sprinkle with lemon juice. Dust with flour.

1/3 cup/75 mL vegetable oil

Fry scallops in oil in a skillet for 3-4 minutes per side until slightly brown, then remove from skillet and put on individual plates.

horseradish butter *(see below)*
2 1/2 cups/625 mL cooked long grain white rice *(to accompany)*

Serve with 1 1/2 tbsp./20 mL horse-radish butter on top of scallops on each plate. Serve immediately. Serve with rice.

Horseradish Butter:

5 tbsp./75 mL butter
— at room temperature
1 1/2 tbsp./20 mL horseradish
juice of 1/2 lemon
3 drops of Worcestershire sauce
1 tbsp./15 mL dry white wine
1 1/2 tbsp./20 mL finely chopped fresh parsley
salt *(to taste)*
white pepper *(to taste)*

Put butter, horseradish, lemon juice, Worcestershire sauce, white wine, parsley, salt and pepper in a mixing bowl and whip for approximately 10 minutes until butter triples in volume. Make horseradish butter in advance of cooking recipe above and store in refrigerator until ready to use.

Leftover horseradish butter may be frozen and used at some other time.

SAUTEED SCALLOPS IN VERMOUTH
Capesante al Vino Bianco

Serves 4

1 1/2 lbs./700 g fresh scallops salt *(to taste)* white pepper *(to taste)* juice of 1 lemon flour *(to dust)*	*Rinse scallops under cold running water and set aside to drain. Season with salt and pepper. Sprinkle with lemon juice. Dust with flour.*
1/3 cup/75 mL olive oil	*Sauté scallops in oil in a skillet for 3-4 minutes per side, then remove from skillet, put on a platter, set aside and keep warm. Drain oil from skillet.*
1 tbsp./15 mL peeled and finely chopped shallots 1/2 cup/125 mL dry white vermouth	*Sauté shallots in vermouth in skillet until vermouth has reduced by one-third.*
3 tbsp./45 mL butter	*Add butter to skillet and blend in.*
juice of 1/2 lemon	*Add lemon juice to skillet and blend in.*
salt *(to taste)* white pepper *(to taste)*	*Season with salt and pepper.*
	Return scallops to skillet and heat for approximately 2 minutes.
2 1/2 cups/625 mL cooked rice pilaf — or saffron rice *(to accompany)*	*Make a bed of rice on individual plates. Spoon contents of skillet over rice on plates and serve immediately.*

SCAMPI
Scampi

Background: *Scampi are small spiny lobsters, cousins to the crayfish, sometimes known as Dublin Bay prawns or Norway lobsters. They are found in the Atlantic ocean off the coast of France, Spain and Portugal, in the north Adriatic Sea, where they are a specialty of Venice, and in the North Atlantic, off Iceland, from where they are exported as Icelandic scampi. Scampi are the size of prawns and are orange in colour. They have white-tipped claws and legs and their colour does not change in cooking. Scampi are prestigious shellfish and are very expensive. Their meat is delicate and precious. They are available, fresh, but, more likely, frozen, all year round.*

BROILED SCAMPI
Scampi alla Griglia

Serves 4

2 lbs./1 kg fresh or frozen scampi, thawed, if frozen, and cut in half lengthwise, with the shells left on — 32 scampi
salt *(to taste)*
freshly ground black pepper *(to taste)*
juice of 1 lemon
1 tsp./5 mL peeled and finely chopped garlic
1/8 tsp./pinch of paprika
1/2 cup/125 mL melted butter
fresh fine white breadcrumbs *(to sprinkle)*

Rinse scampi under cold running water and set aside to drain. Season with salt and pepper and put on a buttered baking tray. Sprinkle with lemon juice, garlic and paprika. Drizzle with butter, then sprinkle with breadcrumbs.

Pre-heat oven to broil/grill.

Put baking tray in oven and broil/grill for 3-5 minutes until scampi are done.

2 tbsp./30 mL finely chopped fresh parsley
1/2 cup/125 mL melted butter *(to accompany)*

Remove baking tray from oven and arrange scampi on a platter. Sprinkle with parsley and serve immediately. Serve directly from platter to individual plates. Serve with melted butter in finger bowls on the side.

SAUTEED SCAMPI WITH ARTICHOKES, SHALLOTS AND WHITE WINE
Scampi Ubriachi

Serves 4

2 lbs./1 kg fresh or frozen scampi, thawed, if frozen, peeled and deveined — 32 scampi
salt *(to taste)*
white pepper *(to taste)*
juice of 1 lemon
flour *(to dust)*

Rinse scampi under cold running water and set aside to drain. Season with salt and pepper. Sprinkle with lemon juice. Dust with flour. Set aside.

4 fresh artichokes, stemmed, with the spiky tips trimmed and any brown outer leaves removed — or 1 (14 oz./398 mL) can of artichoke hearts, drained
juice of 1 lemon
cold water *(to cover 3/4)*
2 tbsp./30 mL salt

Squeeze lemon juice over the tops and bottoms of fresh artichokes, then stand them upright in a stainless steel or enamel saucepan large enough to contain them. Cover artichokes three-quarters with water. Add salt to water and bring to a boil. Reduce heat and cook for 25-35 minutes until artichokes are tender, but firm. Drain pot and rinse artichokes under cold running water. Set artichokes aside and allow them to cool. When artichokes are cool, halve them and clean them of spiny parts and hair. Discard leaves and cut hearts into wedges — or use canned artichoke hearts and cut into wedges. Set aside.

1/4 cup/50 mL olive oil
2 tbsp./30 mL butter

Sauté scampi in oil and butter in a skillet for approximately 2 minutes, then remove from skillet, put on a platter, set aside and keep warm.

Add artichoke hearts to skillet.

2 tbsp./30 mL peeled and finely chopped shallots
1/3 cup/75 mL dry white wine

Add shallots and white wine to skillet and bring to a boil. Reduce heat and simmer for 3-4 minutes.

3 tbsp./45 mL butter

Add butter to skillet and blend in.

Return scampi to skillet. Toss and heat for 1-2 minutes.

1 tbsp./15 mL finely chopped fresh chervil

Transfer contents of skillet to a platter. Sprinkle with chervil and serve immediately. Serve directly from platter to individual plates.

SHRIMP
Gamberetti

Background: *Shrimp are the most used of all crustaceans, followed by crab and lobster. Often, shrimp are confused with prawns and the names are used interchangeably. In the Pacific ocean, there are 85 species of shrimp and prawns, of which six are harvested commercially. Two of these have the highest value: the spot prawn, or spot shrimp, which has a distinctive white spot on the first and fifth segments of its body; and the sidestripe shrimp, so named for the stripes on its abdomen. Both shrimp are available all year round, fresh and frozen. In the Atlantic ocean, pink shrimp are the main species. They are named for their pinky-red colour. They come in an average length, before cleaning, of 4-5 inches/8-10 cm and are available in the spring through fall, fresh and frozen. All shrimp are low in fat content. They are generally sold cleaned and cooked.*

BAKED SHRIMP WITH RICE AND PEAS   Serves 4
Gamberetti con Riso e Piselli

1 lb./500 g fresh baby shrimp

Put shrimp in a bowl and set aside.

1/2 medium onion, peeled and finely chopped
4 tbsp./60 mL butter

Sauté onion in butter in a stovetop-to-oven casserole dish for 2-3 minutes until onion is soft and transparent.

2 1/2 cups/625 mL long grain white rice

Add rice to casserole dish and stir to coat with butter.

3 1/2 cups/875 mL chicken stock (see p. 7)

Add chicken stock to casserole dish.

1/8 tsp./pinch of salt
1/8 tsp./pinch of freshly ground black pepper
1 bay leaf
1 sprig of fresh thyme

Season with salt, pepper, bay leaf and thyme.

Pre-heat oven to 300°F/150°C.

Bring chicken stock to a boil on top of the stove. Stir rice once, reduce heat and cover casserole dish.

Put casserole dish in oven and bake for approximately 15 minutes.

Remove casserole dish from oven and uncover. Add shrimp to dish and gently mix together.

1 cup/250 mL shelled fresh peas 2 tbsp./30 mL butter	*Add peas and butter to dish and gently mix together. Re-cover dish and return to oven. Bake for an additional 5 minutes.*
	Remove casserole dish from oven and serve immediately. Serve directly from casserole dish to individual plates.

GRATINEED SHRIMP
Gamberetti alla Parmigiana

Serves 4

1 1/2 lbs./700 g fresh baby shrimp salt *(to taste)* white pepper *(to taste)* juice of 1/2 lemon	*Put shrimp in a bowl and season with salt and pepper. Sprinkle with lemon juice and set aside.*
3 cups/750 mL white wine sauce *(see p. 12)*	*Put white wine sauce in a saucepan and bring to a boil, then reduce heat.*
3 tbsp./45 mL whipping cream 3 tbsp./45 mL freshly grated Parmesan cheese	*Add cream and Parmesan cheese to saucepan and blend in. Simmer contents of saucepan for approximately 3 minutes, then remove saucepan from heat.*
2 egg yolks	*Add egg yolks to saucepan and blend in.*
	Add shrimp to saucepan and stir in.
3 tbsp./45 mL chopped fresh chives	*Add chives to saucepan and stir in.*
	Pre-heat oven to broil/grill.
	Transfer contents of saucepan to a buttered casserole dish.
4 tbsp./60 mL freshly grated Parmesan cheese 2 tbsp./30 mL chopped fresh chives	*Sprinkle with Parmesan cheese and chives.*
	Put casserole dish in oven and broil/grill until golden brown.
toasted French bread *(to accompany)*	*Remove casserole dish from oven and serve immediately. Serve directly from casserole dish to individual plates. Serve with toasted French bread.*

ARTICHOKES STUFFED WITH SHRIMP   *Serves 4*
Carciofi Ripieni di Gamberetti

1 lb./500 g fresh shrimp

Put shrimp in a bowl and set aside.

4 fresh artichokes, stemmed, with the spiky tips trimmed and any brown outer leaves removed
juice of 1 lemon
cold water *(to cover 3/4)*
2 tbsp./30 mL salt

Squeeze lemon juice over the tops and bottoms of artichokes, then stand them upright in a stainless steel or enamel saucepan large enough to contain them. Cover artichokes three-quarters with water. Add salt to water and bring to a boil. Reduce heat and cook for 20-25 minutes — until just firm. Drain pot and rinse artichokes under cold running water. Set artichokes aside and allow them to cool. When artichokes are cool, carefully clean them by scooping out spiny parts and hair. Rinse artichoke shells thoroughly and put on a baking tray.

Pre-heat oven to 350°F/180°C.

1/4 cup/50 mL Béchamel sauce *(see p. 8)*
3 tbsp./45 mL dry white wine
juice of 1 lime
3 tbsp./45 mL crumbled Gorgonzola cheese
1 tbsp./15 mL freshly grated Parmesan cheese
2 tbsp./30 mL mayonnaise
1 tbsp./15 mL finely chopped fresh basil
1 tsp./5 mL finely chopped fresh oregano
salt *(to taste)*
white pepper *(to taste)*

Put Béchamel sauce, white wine, lime juice, Gorgonzola cheese, Parmesan cheese, mayonnaise, basil, oregano, salt and pepper in a bowl and mix together.

Add shrimp to bowl and mix together thoroughly.

Spoon shrimp mixture into artichoke shells on baking tray.

Put baking tray in the oven and bake for approximately 20 minutes.

herbed mayonnaise *(see p. 14)*
(to accompany)

Remove baking tray from oven and put stuffed artichokes on individual plates. Serve hot or cold. Serve with herbed mayonnaise in a bowl on the side.

SQUID
Calamari

Background: *Squid, or calamari, is a great delicacy that is inexpensive and versatile. Squid have long been popular in the Mediterranean and are gaining popularity in North America, particularly among people who have travelled in Europe. Squid have tubular bodies, or sacs, and 10 arms, or tentacles. They are classified as molluscs. Their colour varies, but their background colour is usually white, with tiny purplish, red to brown dots. Squid vary in length as well — up to 12-18 inches/30-46 cm, including tentacles. They are low in fat content and are available fresh from April to October. They come whole or cleaned — so do not be put off by the thought of cleaning them. They are also available frozen.*

BAKED STUFFED SQUID
Calamari Ripieni

Serves 4

2 1/2-3 lbs./1.25-1.5 kg fresh squid — 20-24 squid	*Clean squid by pulling off the head and pulling out the entrails. Discard head and entrails. Remove quill from squid and discard. Lay squid on a cutting board or flat surface and, using a sharp knife, scrape the membrane off. Rinse squid thoroughly under cold running water. Cut off tentacles in front of eyes, chop and set aside. Make sure beak-like mouth is discarded. Reserve body and set aside for stuffing. Pat body dry with a cloth or paper towel.*
1 medium onion, peeled and finely chopped 1/4 cup/50 mL olive oil	*Sauté onion in oil in a skillet for 2-3 minutes until soft and transparent.*
1 tsp./5 mL peeled and finely chopped garlic	*Add garlic to skillet and sauté for approximately 1 minute.*
	Add chopped squid tentacles to skillet and sauté for 4-5 minutes, then set skillet aside.
6 firm, ripe tomatoes, eyes removed and scored ''x'' on top	*Blanch tomatoes in a pot of rapidly boiling water for 20 seconds, then plunge into a pot of cold water to stop the cooking. Peel, seed and finely chop tomatoes.*

(cont'd over)

	Add tomatoes to skillet.
1/2 cup/125 mL olive oil 2 tbsp./30 mL dry red wine 1/2 tsp./2 mL finely chopped fresh oregano	*Add olive oil, red wine and oregano to skillet and simmer for 10-15 minutes.*
salt *(to taste)* freshly ground black pepper *(to taste)*	*Season with salt and pepper. Set skillet aside.*
6 slices of bread — crusts removed and bread cubed 1/2 cup/125 mL milk	*Soak bread in milk, then squeeze bread dry.*
	Add bread to squid-tomato mixture in skillet and mix together thoroughly.
	Fill squid bodies with tomato-bread stuffing and seal ends of squid with a toothpick. Set squid aside.
	Pre-heat oven to 325°F/160°C.
3 cups/750 mL shelled fresh peas	*Blanch peas in a pot of rapidly boiling water for 30 seconds-1 minute, then plunge into a pot of cold water to stop the cooking.*
	Put peas in a buttered baking pan.
1 tbsp./15 mL butter 1 tbsp./15 mL olive oil	*Dot with butter and olive oil.*
	Put stuffed squid on top of peas in baking pan.
	Put pan in oven and bake for 15-20 minutes.
	Remove baking pan from oven and arrange squid, on top of peas, on a platter. Serve immediately. Serve directly from platter to individual plates.

JULIENNE OF SQUID WITH PEAS
Calamari con Pisellini

Serves 4

2 1/2-3 lbs./1.25-1.5 kg fresh squid
— 20-24 squid
salt *(to taste)*
white pepper *(to taste)*
flour *(to dust)*

Clean squid by pulling off the head and pulling out the entrails. Discard head and entrails. Remove quill from squid and discard. Lay squid on a cutting board or flat surface and, using a sharp knife, scrape the membrane off. Rinse squid thoroughly under cold running water. Cut off tentacles in front of eyes and reserve. Make sure beak-like mouth is discarded. Chop tentacles, if large. Chop body into 1/4 inch/6 mm rounds. Pat squid dry with a cloth or paper towel. Season with salt and pepper. Dust with flour and set aside.

1/4 lb./125 g pancetta (Italian bacon), julienned
1/2 medium onion, peeled and diced
3 tbsp./45 mL olive oil

Sauté pancetta and onion in oil in a skillet for 2-3 minutes until onion is soft and transparent, then set skillet aside.

1/4 cup/50 mL olive oil

Sauté squid in oil in a separate skillet for 3-4 minutes until golden brown.

Add pancetta and onion to skillet with squid and mix together.

3 cups/750 mL drained canned petits pois

Add petits pois to skillet and sauté for approximately 5 minutes.

2 cups/500 mL washed and julienned iceberg lettuce

Add lettuce to skillet. Toss and heat.

salt *(to taste)*
white pepper *(to taste)*

Season with salt and pepper.

Transfer contents of skillet to a platter and serve immediately. Serve directly from platter to individual plates.

PAN-FRIED SQUID RINGS
SERVED WITH LEMON HALVES
Calamari Fritti all' Italiana

Serves 4

2 1/2-3 lbs./1.25-1.5 kg fresh squid
— 20-24 squid
salt *(to taste)*
freshly ground black pepper *(to taste)*
juice of 1/2 lemon
1/2 tsp./2 mL peeled and
finely chopped garlic
2 cups/500 mL flour
— seasoned with 1 tbsp./
15 mL paprika

Clean squid by pulling off the head and pulling out the entrails. Discard head and entrails. Remove quill from squid and discard. Lay squid on a cutting board or flat surface and using a sharp knife, scrape the membrane off. Rinse squid thoroughly under cold running water. Cut off tentacles in front of eyes and reserve. Make sure beak-like mouth is discarded. Chop tentacles, if large. Chop body into 1/2-1 inch/1-2 cm rounds. Pat squid dry with a cloth or paper towel. Season with salt and pepper. Sprinkle with lemon juice and garlic. Dredge in flour.

4 cups/1 L vegetable oil

Fry squid, a few at a time, in oil in a skillet for approximately 1 minute until golden brown, then remove from skillet and drain on paper towels. Put squid on a platter, set aside and keep warm. Do not overcrowd squid in skillet.

2 lemons, cut in half

Transfer squid to individual warm plates and serve immediately. Serve with lemon halves.

SAUTEED SQUID
WITH A CONCASSE OF TOMATOES
Calamari al Pomodoro

Serves 4

2 1/2-3 lbs./1.25-1.5 kg fresh squid
— 20-24 squid
salt *(to taste)*
freshly ground black pepper *(to taste)*
1/2 tsp./2 mL peeled and
finely chopped garlic
flour *(to dust)*

Clean squid by pulling off the head and pulling out the entrails. Discard head and entrails. Remove quill from squid and discard. Lay squid on a cutting board or flat surface and, using a sharp knife, scrape the membrane off. Rinse squid thoroughly under cold running water. Cut off tentacles in front of eyes and reserve. Make sure beak-like mouth is discarded. Chop tentacles, if large. Chop body into 1/2-1 inch/1-2 cm rounds. Pat squid dry with a cloth or paper towel. Season with salt and pepper. Sprinkle with garlic. Dust with flour and set aside.

8 firm, ripe tomatoes, eyes removed
and scored ''x'' on top

Blanch tomatoes in a pot of rapidly boiling water for 20 seconds, then plunge into a pot of cold water to stop the cooking. Peel, seed and chop concassé tomatoes. Set aside.

1/4 cup/50 mL olive oil
1 tbsp./15 mL butter

Sauté squid in oil and butter in a skillet for 3-4 minutes until golden brown.

2 tbsp./30 mL peeled and
finely chopped shallots
1 tsp./5 mL peeled and
finely chopped garlic
1 tbsp./15 mL finely chopped
fresh basil
1 tbsp./15 mL finely chopped
fresh oregano

Add shallots, garlic, basil and oregano to skillet and simmer for 1-2 minutes.

Add tomatoes to skillet and simmer for 2-3 minutes.

4 tbsp./60 mL extra virgin olive oil

Add olive oil to skillet and blend in.

freshly ground black pepper *(to taste)*
1 tbsp./15 mL finely chopped
fresh basil

Transfer contents of skillet to a platter. Sprinkle with pepper and basil and serve immediately. Serve directly from platter to individual plates.

SAUTEED SQUID WITH ARTICHOKES
Calamari alla Giudea

Serves 4

2 1/2-3 lbs./1.25-1.5 kg fresh squid
— 20-24 squid
salt *(to taste)*
freshly ground black pepper *(to taste)*
1/2 tsp./2 mL peeled and
finely chopped garlic
flour *(to dust)*

Clean squid by pulling off the head and pulling out the entrails. Discard head and entrails. Remove quill from squid and discard. Lay squid on a cutting board or flat surface and, using a sharp knife, scrape the membrane off. Rinse squid thoroughly under cold running water. Cut off tentacles in front of eyes and reserve. Make sure beak-like mouth is discarded. Chop tentacles, if large. Chop body into 1/2-1 inch/1-2 cm rounds. Pat squid dry with a cloth or paper towel. Season with salt and pepper. Sprinkle with garlic. Dust with flour and set aside.

4 fresh artichokes, stemmed,
with the spiky tips trimmed and
any brown outer leaves removed
1 lemon, cut in half
1/2 cup/125 mL olive oil

Squeeze lemon juice over artichokes, then cut them in half. Carefully clean them of spiny parts and hair, then cut each half into 6-8 wedges, snapping or pulling off the outer leaves. Fry artichoke wedges in oil in a skillet for approximately 5 minutes until tender, then remove from skillet, put on a platter, set aside and keep warm. Drain oil from skillet.

1/4 cup/50 mL olive oil
1 tbsp./15 mL butter

Put oil and butter in skillet.

Sauté squid in oil and butter in skillet for 3-4 minutes until golden brown, then drain oil from skillet.

Return artichoke wedges to skillet.

1/4 cup/50 mL dry white wine
juice of 1 lemon
3 tbsp./45 mL chicken stock
(see p. 7)
3 tbsp./45 mL extra virgin olive oil

Add white wine, lemon juice, chicken stock and olive oil to skillet and simmer for 3-4 minutes.

3 tbsp./45 mL finely chopped
fresh parsley

Transfer contents of skillet to a platter. Sprinkle with parsley and serve immediately. Serve directly from platter to individual plates.

COD
Merluzzo

Background: *Cod are probably the best-known fish in the world and are one of the most-used fish in the ocean because they are widely available. Cod are extremely servicable, adaptable to any cooking method. With their mild flavour and their white flesh, which flakes easily, they are always popular. Cod are found in both the Pacific and Atlantic oceans, but they are often confused with other fish. On the Pacific coast, rock, ling and black cod, or Alaska black cod, are all marketed as cod, but they are not true cod. Pacific cod, or grey cod, are brown to grey on their backs, with lighter sides and bellies shading to grey or white. They have a distinctive barbel on their chins and range in weight from 3-8 lbs./1.5-4 kg. True cod are low in fat content and they are usually sold as fillets. Atlantic cod are more elongated than Pacific cod and vary in colour from grey to green and brown to red, with a pale lateral line, whitish bellies and the same distinctive barbel on their chins. They average about 5 lbs./2.5 kg in weight. Cod should not be confused with the Pacific hake or whiting, or silver hake and red hake of the Atlantic, which are members of the cod family; the pollock of both the Pacific and the Atlantic, another member of the cod family; the haddock of the Atlantic, which, too, is a member of the cod family; the sablefish or black cod of the Pacific, which is not a cod; and the ling cod of the Pacific, which is a greenling.*

BAKED FILLET OF COD WITH LEEKS   *Serves 4*
Merluzzo Arrosto con Porri

4 (6-8 oz./175-250 g) fillets of fresh cod
salt *(to taste)*
white pepper *(to taste)*
juice of 1/2 lemon
dash of Worcestershire sauce
dash of Tabasco sauce
4 tsp./20 mL butter

Rinse fillets of cod under cold running water and pat dry with paper towels. Season with salt and pepper and put in a buttered baking dish. Sprinkle with lemon juice, Worcestershire sauce and Tabasco sauce. Dab 1 tsp./5 mL butter on top of each fillet.

Pre-heat oven to 400°F/200°C.

(cont'd over)

Put baking dish in oven and bake for 15-18 minutes until fish is done, then remove dish from oven, put fillets on a platter, side aside and keep warm. Reserve liquid in baking dish.

1 medium leek, halved, washed and sliced — use the white part and some of the light green
3 tbsp./45 mL dry white wine
juice of 1 lemon
baking liquid (reserved above)

Sauté leek in white wine, lemon juice and baking liquid in a skillet for approximately 2 minutes.

4 tbsp./60 mL butter

Add butter to skillet and blend in.

salt (to taste)
white pepper (to taste)

Season with salt and pepper.

Spoon contents of skillet over fillets of cod on platter and serve immediately. Serve directly from platter to individual plates.

COD STEW WITH
SCALLOPED POTATOES AND ARTICHOKES Serves 4
Spezzatino di Merluzzo con Patate e Carciofi

1 1/2 lbs./700 g fillet of fresh cod, bones removed — cut into 1 inch/ 2 cm cubes
salt (to taste)
freshly ground black pepper (to taste)

Rinse cubes of cod under cold running water and pat dry with paper towels. Season with salt and pepper and set aside.

5-6 medium potatoes, peeled and thinly sliced
cold water (to cover)

Soak potatoes in a pot of cold water, then drain pot and pat potatoes dry. Set aside.

2 medium onions, peeled and thinly sliced — separated into rings

Put onions in a bowl and set aside.

4 fresh artichokes, stemmed, with the spiky tips trimmed and any brown outer leaves removed — or 1 (14 oz./398 mL) can of artichoke hearts, drained
juice of 1 lemon
cold water (to cover 3/4)
2 tbsp./30 mL salt

Squeeze lemon juice over the tops and bottoms of fresh artichokes, then stand them upright in a stainless steel or enamel saucepan large enough to contain them. Cover artichokes three-quarters with water. Add salt to water and bring to a boil. Reduce heat and cook for 25-35 minutes until artichokes are tender, but firm. Drain pot and rinse artichokes under cold running water.

Set artichokes aside and allow them to cool. When artichokes are cool, halve them and clean them of spiny parts and hair. Discard leaves and cut hearts into wedges — or use canned artichoke hearts and cut into wedges. Set aside.

Pre-heat oven to 400°F/200°C.

salt *(to taste)* per layer freshly ground black pepper *(to taste)* per layer 1/8 tsp./pinch of ground nutmeg per layer 1 tbsp./15 mL butter per layer	Layer 1 (9 x 9 inch/23 x 23 cm) buttered baking dish with potatoes, onions, artichokes and cod, in that order, until all ingredients are used up. Season each layer with salt, pepper and nutmeg and dab each layer with butter. Set aside.
1 1/2 cups/375 mL milk 1 cup/250 mL chicken stock *(see p. 7)*	Mix milk and chicken stock together in a bowl and pour over ingredients in baking dish.
4 tbsp./60 mL freshly grated Parmesan cheese	Sprinkle with Parmesan cheese.
	Put baking dish in oven and bake for 30-40 minutes.
1 tbsp./15 mL finely chopped fresh parsley	Remove baking dish from oven and sprinkle with parsley. Serve immediately. Serve directly from baking dish to individual bowls.

PAN-FRIED FILLET OF COD WITH PIZZAIOLA SAUCE
Filetti di Merluzzo Fritti Salsa Pizzaiola

Serves 4

4 (6-8 oz./175-250 g) fillets of fresh cod salt *(to taste)* white pepper *(to taste)* juice of 1/2 lemon dash of Worcestershire sauce flour *(to coat)*	Rinse fillets of cod under cold running water and pat dry with paper towels. Season with salt and pepper. Sprinkle with lemon juice and Worcestershire sauce. Dredge in flour.
1/4 cup/50 mL vegetable oil 2 tbsp./30 mL butter	Fry cod in oil and butter in skillet for 4-5 minutes per side until golden brown, then remove from skillet, put on a platter, set aside and keep warm. Drain oil from skillet.

(cont'd over)

2 tbsp./30 mL dry white wine	*Deglaze skillet with white wine.*
1 1/2 cups/375 mL pizzaiola sauce (see p. 101)	*Add pizzaiola sauce to skillet and simmer for approximately 2 minutes.*
1 tbsp./15 mL extra virgin olive oil	*Add olive oil to skillet and blend in.*
1 tbsp./15 mL finely chopped fresh parsley	*Spoon contents of skillet over fillets of cod on platter. Sprinkle with parsley and serve immediately. Serve directly from platter to individual plates.*

SAUTEED SCALLOPS OF COD WITH MUSHROOMS AND THYME   *Serves 4*
Fette di Merluzzo con Funghi e Timo

1 1/2 lbs./700 g fillet of fresh cod — cut into 1 inch/2 cm scallops salt *(to taste)* white pepper *(to taste)* juice of 1 lemon flour *(to dust)*	*Rinse scallops of cod under cold running water and pat dry with paper towels. Season with salt and pepper. Sprinkle with lemon juice. Dust with flour.*
1/4 cup/50 mL vegetable oil 2 tbsp./30 mL butter	*Sauté cod in oil and butter in a skillet for 2-3 minutes per side until golden brown, then remove from skillet, put on a platter, set aside and keep warm. Reserve oil in skillet.*
2 cups/500 mL cleaned and thinly sliced fresh mushrooms	*Add mushrooms to skillet and sauté for 1-2 minutes.*
1/2 cup/125 mL dry white wine juice of 1 lemon 1 tbsp./15 mL fresh thyme	*Add white wine, lemon juice and thyme to skillet and simmer for approximately 3 minutes.*
2 tbsp./30 mL whipping cream	*Add cream to skillet, blend in and simmer for approximately 2 minutes.*
4 tbsp./60 mL butter	*Add butter to skillet and blend in.*
salt *(to taste)* white pepper *(to taste)*	*Season with salt and pepper.*
1 tbsp./15 mL finely chopped fresh parsley 1 lemon, cut into 4 wedges	*Spoon contents of skillet over scallops of cod on platter. Sprinkle with parsley. Garnish platter with lemon wedges and serve immediately. Serve directly from platter to individual plates.*

STEAMED COD
WITH OLIVE OIL AND LEMON JUICE *Serves 4*
Merluzzo al Vapore

4 (6-8 oz./175-250 g) fillets of fresh cod
salt *(to taste)*
freshly ground black pepper *(to taste)*
1 tsp./5 mL finely chopped fresh basil
1/4 tsp./1 mL finely chopped fresh oregano
1/2 tsp./2 mL finely chopped fresh tarragon
1/2 tsp./2 mL peeled and finely chopped garlic
1/4 cup/50 mL seeded and finely chopped green pepper
2 tbsp./30 mL marinated sundried tomatoes, drained and finely chopped
8 thin slices of lemon
8 tbsp./120 mL extra virgin olive oil

Rinse fillets of cod under cold running water and pat dry with paper towels. Season with salt and pepper and put in a buttered baking pan. Sprinkle with basil, oregano, tarragon, garlic, green pepper and sundried tomatoes.
Put 2 slices of lemon on top of each fillet and drizzle with 2 tbsp./30 mL olive oil per fillet.

Pre-heat oven to 400°F/200°C.

1/4 cup/50 mL chicken stock (see p. 7)
2 tbsp./30 mL dry white wine

Add chicken stock and white wine to baking pan and bring to a boil on top of the stove.

buttered paper

Cover baking pan with a sheet of buttered paper. Put pan in oven and steam for 15 minutes, then remove pan from oven and put fillets on a platter.

2 tbsp./30 mL extra virgin olive oil

Drizzle fillets of cod on platter with olive oil and serve immediately. Serve directly from platter to individual plates.

SALT COD
Baccala

Background: *Historical records indicate that cod has been cured from the time of the Vikings in the 8th century. Before refrigeration, salt cod was one of the few fish that was known to people who did not live on the ocean. Cod lends itself to curing better than any other fish because it holds out against decay longer than any other fish, sometimes for years. Although salt cod is not as popular as it used to be, it should not be forgotten.*

BAKED SALT COD WITH ONIONS AND POTATOES
Serves 4
Baccala con Cipolla e Patate

1 1/2 lbs./700 g fillet of dried salt cod
cold water *(to cover)*

Soak cod in a pan of cold water for 12-24 hours, depending on cure. Drain pan and cut cod into 1 inch/2 cm cubes. Return cod to pan and cover with water. Bring water to a boil on top of stove and skim. Reduce heat and poach cod for approximately 15 minutes, then drain pan, reserving the liquid, and set cod and liquid aside.

6-8 medium potatoes, peeled and thinly sliced

Soak potatoes in a pot of cold water, then drain pot and pat potatoes dry. Set aside.

1 1/2 medium onions, peeled and thinly sliced — separated into rings

Put onions in a bowl and set aside.

Pre-heat oven to 400°F/200°C.

freshly ground black pepper *(to taste)* per layer
1/8 tsp./pinch of ground nutmeg per layer
1/2 tbsp./7 mL butter per layer

Layer 1 (9 x 9 inch/23 x 23 cm) buttered baking dish with potatoes, onions and cod, in that order, until ingredients are used up. Season each layer with pepper and nutmeg and dab each layer with butter.

poaching liquid from salt cod *(reserved above — to cover 3/4)*

Add poaching liquid from cod to baking dish to cover three-quarters.

buttered paper *(optional)*

Put baking dish in oven and bake for 45-60 minutes. Watch colour of fish while baking. If fish begins to darken, cover pan with a sheet of buttered paper.

Remove baking dish from oven and serve immediately. Serve directly from baking dish to individual plates.

BRAISED SALT COD WITH TOMATOES, BLACK OLIVES AND SILVER ONIONS
Baccala in Umido

Serves 4

1 1/2 lbs./700 g fillet of dried salt cod cold water *(to cover)*	*Soak cod in a pan of cold water for 12-24 hours, depending on cure. Drain pan and cut cod into 2 inch/ 5 cm cubes. Return cod to pan and cover with water. Bring water to a boil on top of stove and skim. Reduce heat and poach cod for approximately 15 minutes, then drain pan and set cod aside.*
1 1/2 cups/375 mL silver onions 1/4 cup/50 mL olive oil	*Sauté onions in oil in a pot for 3-5 minutes.*
2 (28 oz./796 mL) cans of drained, crushed, peeled Italian plum tomatoes — crushed by hand 1/2 tsp./2 mL peeled and finely chopped garlic 2 tsp./10 mL finely chopped fresh parsley	*Add tomatoes, garlic and parsley to pot and mix together.*
1 tsp./5 mL finely chopped fresh basil 1/2 tsp./2 mL finely chopped fresh oregano 1/2 tsp./2 mL chopped fresh rosemary 1/2 tsp./2 mL fresh thyme freshly ground black pepper *(to taste)*	*Season with basil, oregano, rosemary, thyme and pepper.*
	Add cod to pot and bring to a boil. Reduce heat, cover pot and cook for approximately 15 minutes until cod is tender.
4 tbsp./60 mL pitted, sliced Calamata black olives	*Uncover pot and add olives to pot. Re-cover pot and cook for an additional 2 minutes.*
	Check seasoning and adjust, if necessary.
	Transfer contents of pot to a platter or individual plates and serve immediately.

EEL
Anguilla

Background: *Eel breed in saltwater and they live either in shallow coastal water or in freshwater. They have long been popular in Europe, but, in North America, they are not well known. Perhaps their problem is their resemblance to snakes. If they are thought of as elongated fish, which they are, perhaps they would be more popular. Their flesh is firm and white and they have a delicious flavour. Eel are available fresh, and live, in tanks; they are also available smoked. In the Atlantic ocean, where eel are common, they are known by various names such as: silver eel, brown eel, yellow eel and anguille commune. Eel are black to muddy brown above, with yellow sides and yellowish-white bellies. They range in size from 3-4 feet/ 72-96 cm and weigh 2-3 lbs./1-1.5 kg. They are caught in traps in rivers and estuaries and are available fresh from August to November. Eel are high in fat content and are highly perishable. They are best kept alive until just before cooking.*

PAN-FRIED MEDALLIONS OF EEL   *Serves 4*
Anguilla Dorata

2 lbs./1 kg fresh eel, cleaned and skinned — cut into 2 inch/5 cm pieces
salt *(to taste)*
freshly ground black pepper *(to taste)*

Rinse eel under cold running water and pat dry with paper towels. Season with salt and pepper and set aside.

3 eggs, beaten

Put eggs in a bowl and set aside.

6 tbsp./90 mL fresh fine white breadcrumbs
6 tbsp./90 mL freshly grated Parmesan cheese

Mix breadcrumbs and Parmesan cheese together in a bowl and set aside.

Dip eel in eggs, then roll in breadcrumbs to coat.

1/2 cup/125 mL olive oil

Fry eel in oil in a skillet for 5-6 minutes until golden brown, then remove from skillet and drain on paper towels.

salt *(to taste)*
freshly ground black pepper *(to taste)*
1 tsp./5 mL finely chopped fresh sage
1 tsp./5 mL finely chopped fresh rosemary
2 lemons, cut into 8 wedges

Put eel on a platter and season with salt and pepper. Sprinkle with sage and rosemary. Garnish platter with lemon wedges and serve immediately. Serve directly from platter to individual plates.

FLOUNDER
Passera

Background: *Flounder is the collective name of a number of individual Atlantic ocean flatfish: the summer flounder or fluke; the winter flounder, which is sometimes known as the blackback, the lemon sole or the Georges Bank flounder; the witch flounder or gray sole, also known as the pale flounder, the pole dab and the white sole; the yellowtail flounder or rusty dab; and the American plaice, which is also known as the Canadian plaice, the roughback, the dab, the sand dab or, simply, plaice. All flounders live offshore, except for the winter flounder, which can be found inshore. Flounders vary in weight, from 1 1/2 lbs./700 g average for witch or yellowtail flounder, 2-3 lbs./1-1.5 kg average for plaice and 3 lbs./1.5 kg average for winter flounder, to 14 lbs./7 kg average for summer flounder, the largest of the species. Flounder are available fresh from February to October and are sold, for the most part, as fillets. They have soft white flesh and are low in fat content. They are a very popular East Coast fish. Although some flounders are known as sole, they are not to be confused with sole, which is a different fish, although the two fish can be used similarly.*

BAKED FILLET OF FLOUNDER WITH GOLDEN CAVIAR AND GRAPPA BUTTER   *Serves 4*
Filetti di Passera con Caviale e Burro di Grappa

4 (6-8 oz./175-250 g) fillets of fresh flounder
salt *(to taste)*
white pepper *(to taste)*
2 tbsp./30 mL grappa
1/4 cup/50 mL milk
2 drops of Worcestershire sauce
fresh fine white breadcrumbs *(to coat)*
4 tsp./20 mL melted butter

Rinse fillets of flounder under cold running water and pat dry with paper towels. Season with salt and pepper. Sprinkle with grappa, then sprinkle with milk and Worcestershire sauce. Roll in breadcrumbs. Press breadcrumbs onto flounder. Put fillets in a buttered baking dish and drizzle with 1 tsp./5 mL butter per fillet.

Pre-heat oven to 450°F/230°C.

Put baking dish in oven and bake for 7-8 minutes, then remove dish from oven and put fillets on a platter.

4 tsp./20 mL golden caviar
1 lemon, cut into 4 wedges
grappa butter *(see below)*

Put 1 tsp./5 mL caviar on top of each fillet of flounder on platter. Garnish platter with lemon wedges and serve immediately. Serve directly from platter to individual plates. Serve with grappa butter in a sauceboat on the side.

(cont'd over)

Grappa Butter:

1 tbsp./15 mL peeled and finely chopped shallots 2 tbsp./30 mL grappa juice of 1 lemon	*Sauté shallots in grappa and lemon juice in a saucepan for 1-2 minutes.*
1/2 cup/125 mL butter	*Add butter to saucepan and blend in, then remove saucepan from heat.*
salt *(to taste)* white pepper *(to taste)*	*Season with salt and pepper.*
	Transfer contents of saucepan to a sauceboat and serve warm.

PAN-FRIED FILLET OF FLOUNDER
WITH APPLES AND ALMONDS   Serves 4
Filetti di Passera in Padella con Mele e Mandorla

4 (6-8 oz./175-250 g) fillets of fresh flounder salt *(to taste)* white pepper *(to taste)* juice of 1/2 lemon flour *(to dust)*	*Rinse fillets of flounder under cold running water and pat dry with paper towels. Season with salt and pepper. Sprinkle with lemon juice. Dust with flour.*
1/4 cup/50 mL vegetable oil 2 tbsp./30 mL butter	*Fry flounder in oil and butter in a skillet for 2-3 minutes per side until golden brown, then remove from skillet and drain on paper towels. Put fillets on a platter, set aside and keep warm. Drain oil from skillet.*
1 green apple, peeled, cored and julienned juice of 1 lemon	*Put apple in a bowl and sprinkle with lemon juice.*
4 tbsp./60 mL butter 2 tbsp./30 mL dry white wine	*Sauté apple in butter and white wine in skillet for 1-2 minutes.*
3 tbsp./45 mL toasted sliced almonds	*Add almonds to skillet. Toss and heat.*
juice of 1 lemon	*Sprinkle with lemon juice.*
salt *(to taste)* white pepper *(to taste)*	*Season with salt and pepper.*
1 tbsp./15 mL finely chopped fresh parsley	*Spoon contents of skillet over fillets of flounder on platter. Sprinkle with parsley and serve immediately. Serve directly from platter to individual plates.*

PAN-FRIED FILLET OF FLOUNDER
WITH CUCUMBER SAUCE
Filetti di Passera alla Salsa di Cetrioli

Serves 4

4 (6-8 oz./175-250 g) fillets of fresh flounder

Rinse fillets of flounder under cold running water and pat dry with paper towels. Set aside.

1/2 cup/125 mL fine breadcrumbs
(not necessarily white)
1/4 cup/50 mL flour

Mix breadcrumbs and flour together in a bowl.

salt *(to taste)*
white pepper *(to taste)*

Season with salt and pepper.

Dredge flounder in breadcrumb mixture.

1/4 cup/50 mL vegetable oil
2 tbsp./30 mL butter

Fry flounder in oil and butter in a skillet for 2-3 minutes per side until golden brown, then remove from skillet and drain on paper towels. Put fillets on a platter, set aside and keep warm. Reserve oil in skillet.

1 large shallot,
peeled and finely chopped
1 stalk of celery,
washed, threaded and chopped

Add shallots and celery to skillet and sauté for 1-2 minutes.

1/2 cup/125 mL chicken stock
(see p. 7) — or 1/4 cup/50 mL
dry white wine and 1/4 cup/50 mL
cold water
1 large cucumber,
peeled, seeded and chopped
juice of 1/2 lemon

Add chicken stock or white wine and water, cucumber and lemon juice to skillet and bring to a boil. Reduce heat and simmer for 3-5 minutes, then transfer contents of skillet to a blender and purée. Return cucumber purée to skillet and heat.

2 tbsp./30 mL butter

Add butter to skillet and blend in.

(cont'd over)

Photo #5 *(page 133)*: Shellfish. *Clockwise from left:* Crab Pie; Mussels with Egg and Asparagus Tips; and Pan-Fried Squid Rings Served with Lemon Halves. Quiche dish and cast iron cookware courtesy of Basic Stock Cookware; Mick Henry plate *(foreground)* courtesy of Evelyn Springer.

Photo #6 *(page 134)*: Saltwater Fish. *Clockwise from left:* Cod Stew with Scalloped Potatoes and Artichokes; Pan-Fried Fillet of Flounder with Apples and Almonds; and Baked Fillet of Halibut with Mussels and Saffron Sauce. Le Creuset cookware *(left)* courtesy of Tools & Techniques; plate *(right)* courtesy of W.H. Puddifoot; and cast iron cookware *(foreground)* courtesy of Basic Stock Cookware.

2 tbsp./30 mL finely chopped fresh dill	*Add dill to skillet and stir in.*
4 sprigs of fresh dill	*Transfer contents of skillet to a platter. Garnish each fillet of flounder with 1 sprig of dill and serve immediately. Serve directly from platter to individual plates.*

STEAMED FILLET OF FLOUNDER WITH OREGANO, SAGE AND THYME DRIZZLED WITH EXTRA VIRGIN OLIVE OIL AND SERVED WITH LEMON WEDGES *Serves 4*
Filetti di Passera Lessato Erbe Aromatiche

4 (6-8 oz./175-250 g) fillets of fresh flounder	*Rinse fillets of flounder under cold running water and pat dry with paper towels.*
olive oil *(to coat)*	*Coat the bottom of a baking pan with olive oil.*
salt *(to taste)* white pepper *(to taste)* juice of 1 lemon 2 tbsp./30 mL dry white wine 6 sprigs of fresh oregano 8 medium size leaves of fresh sage 4 sprigs of fresh thyme 4 tbsp./60 mL extra virgin olive oil	*Season flounder with salt and pepper and put in baking pan. Sprinkle with lemon juice and white wine. Put 1 1/2 sprigs of oregano, 2 leaves of sage and 1 sprig of thyme on top of each fillet and drizzle with 1 tbsp./15 mL olive oil per fillet.*
buttered paper	*Cover baking pan with a sheet of buttered paper. Bring to a boil on top of the stove, then reduce heat and steam for 3-5 minutes until fish is done.*
1 tbsp./15 mL extra virgin olive oil 1 lemon, cut into 4 wedges	*Remove fillets of flounder from baking pan and put on a platter. Drizzle with olive oil. Garnish platter with lemon wedges and serve immediately. Serve directly from platter to individual plates.*

HALIBUT
Ippoglosso

Background: *Halibut are the largest of all flatfish and are found in both the Pacific and the Atlantic ocean. They are caught offshore with longlines and range in weight up to 600 lbs./300 kg, but the average landed weight for Pacific halibut is 32 lbs./16 kg and, for Atlantic halibut, between 5-132 lbs./2.5-56 kg. Atlantic halibut are sometimes confused with Greenland halibut or turbot. Halibut are greenish brown to dark brown on their uppersides and white to grey or mottled grey-white on their undersides. Off the Pacific coast, halibut are available fresh from May to November. They are available frozen all year round. Off the Atlantic coast, they are available, fresh and frozen, all year round, but fresh, primarily, from April to June. Halibut are marketed as fillets and steaks. They have moderate fat content and firm, white flesh, which has a delicate flavour. There is no better fish than halibut, particularly at the start of its season. Watch for it to become available fresh and buy some immediately.*

BAKED FILLET OF HALIBUT WITH GREEN GRAPES
Serves 4
Ippoglosso al Forno con Uva Verde

4 (6 oz./175 g) fillets of fresh halibut
salt *(to taste)*
white pepper *(to taste)*

Rinse fillets of halibut under cold running water and pat dry with paper towels. Gently flatten fillets by hand. Season with salt and pepper and put in a buttered baking dish.

Pre-heat oven to 400°F/200°C.

1/2 cup/125 mL dry white vermouth

Add vermouth to baking dish.

Put baking dish in oven and bake for 3-5 minutes.

Remove baking dish from oven and put fillets on a platter. Set aside and keep warm. Reserve liquid in baking dish and transfer to a saucepan. Reduce liquid in saucepan by simmering for approximately 1 minute.

1/3 cup/75 mL whipping cream

Add cream to saucepan, blend in and simmer for 2-3 minutes.

1/3 cup/75 mL peeled and halved seedless green grapes
4 tbsp./60 mL washed and julienned fresh sorrel

Add grapes and sorrel to saucepan and heat, then remove saucepan from heat.

(cont'd over)

3 tbsp./45 mL butter	*Add butter to saucepan and blend in.*
juice of 1/2 lemon	*Add lemon juice to saucepan and blend in.*
salt *(to taste)* white pepper *(to taste)*	*Season with salt and pepper.*
	Spoon contents of saucepan over fillets of halibut on platter and serve immediately. Serve directly from platter to individual plates.

BAKED FILLET OF HALIBUT
WITH MUSSELS AND SAFFRON SAUCE   *Serves 4*
Ippoglosso al Forno alla Moda di Spagna

4 (6-8 oz./175-250 g) fillets of fresh halibut salt *(to taste)* white pepper *(to taste)* juice of 1/2 lemon fresh fine white breadcrumbs *(to coat)* 4 tsp./20 mL melted butter	*Rinse fillets of halibut under cold running water and pat dry with paper towels. Season with salt and pepper. Sprinkle with lemon juice. Dredge in breadcrumbs. Press breadcrumbs onto halibut. Put fillets on a buttered baking tray and drizzle with 1 tsp./5 mL butter per fillet.*
	Pre-heat oven to 400°F/200°C.
	Put baking tray in oven and bake for approximately 15 minutes until fish is done.
3/4 lb./350 g fresh mussels, washed and cleaned 2 tbsp./30 mL dry white wine 1 tbsp./15 mL peeled and finely chopped shallots 1/4 tsp./1 mL peeled and finely chopped garlic	*While halibut is baking, put mussels in a pot with white wine, shallots and garlic. Cover pot and steam mussels for 5-6 minutes until they open. Drain pot, reserving the liquid, and remove mussels from shells, leaving 4 mussels in shells for garnish. Discard any mussels that do not open. Set mussels aside and keep warm. Strain mussel liquid through a sieve lined with a linen or muslin cloth into a saucepan.*
1/8-1/4 tsp./pinch-1 mL saffron threads	*Add saffron to saucepan and simmer for 1-2 minutes.*

1/2 cup/125 mL whipping cream	*Add cream to saucepan, blend in and bring to a boil. Reduce heat and simmer for 2-3 minutes, then remove saucepan from heat.*
4 tbsp./60 mL butter	*Add butter to saucepan and blend in.*
juice of 1/2 lemon	*Add lemon juice to saucepan and blend in.*
salt *(to taste)* white pepper *(to taste)*	*Season with salt and pepper. Set saucepan aside and keep warm.*
4 tsp./20 mL concassé of tomatoes 4 tsp./20 mL chopped fresh chives	*Just before serving sauce, add concassé of tomatoes and chopped chives to saucepan and stir in.*

When halibut has finished baking, remove tray from oven and put fillets on individual plates. Arrange mussels along 1 side of each fillet. Garnish with 1 mussel, in the shell, along other side of fillet.

Spoon sauce in saucepan over one-half of each fillet on plates — the half with 1 mussel in the shell — and serve immediately.

GRILLED HALIBUT STEAK MARINATED IN OLIVE OIL AND FRESH HERBS
Ippoglosso alla Griglia con Erbe Fresche

Serves 4

4 (6-8 oz./175-250 g) fresh halibut steaks	*Rinse halibut steaks under cold running water and pat dry with paper towels.*
marinade *(see below)*	*Put halibut steaks in marinade in a baking dish in the refrigerator overnight, turning steaks several times, then remove dish from refrigerator. Drain halibut and reserve marinade for basting while halibut is barbecuing.*
1/2 lemon	*Put halibut steaks on the oiled rack of a barbecue and cook slowly over hot coals for 7-8 minutes, lightly basting with marinade, squeezing with lemon juice and turning to trellis-mark, until fish is done. Reserve leftover marinade to serve as a sauce and put in a sauceboat.*
1 lemon, cut into 4 wedges extra virgin olive oil or leftover marinade *(reserved above)* *(to accompany)*	*When fish is done, remove from barbecue and put on a platter or individual plates. Garnish platter or plates with lemon wedges and serve immediately. Serve with extra virgin olive oil or leftover marinade in sauceboat on the side.*

Marinade:

1/2 cup/125 mL olive oil 1 clove of garlic, peeled and crushed 1 tbsp./15 mL finely chopped fresh parsley 1 tsp./5 mL freshly ground black pepper 1/2 tsp./2 mL finely chopped fresh basil 1/4 tsp./1 mL finely chopped fresh marjoram 1/4 tsp./1 mL finely chopped fresh oregano 1/4 tsp./1 mL finely chopped fresh tarragon 1/2 tsp./2 mL fresh thyme	*Mix olive oil, garlic, parsley, pepper, basil, marjoram, oregano, tarragon and thyme together in a baking dish.*

PAN-FRIED HALIBUT STEAK
WITH A LIGHT GREEN SAUCE
Bistecca d' Ippoglosso alla Genovese

Serves 4

4 (6-8 oz./175-250 g) fresh halibut steaks salt *(to taste)* freshly ground black pepper *(to taste)* flour *(to dust)*	*Rinse halibut steaks under cold running water and pat dry with paper towels. Season with salt and pepper. Dust with flour.*
1/4 cup/50 mL butter	*Fry halibut steaks in butter in a skillet for 4-5 minutes per side until golden brown, then remove from skillet and put on a platter. Remove skin and centre bone from steaks, if desired, and discard. Set platter aside and keep warm.*
1/4 cup/50 mL dry white wine	*Deglaze skillet with white wine.*
juice of 1 lemon	*Add lemon juice to skillet and blend in.*
1/2 cup/125 mL whipping cream	*Add cream to skillet and blend in. Simmer for 2-3 minutes.*
4 tbsp./60 mL finely chopped fresh basil 2 tbsp./30 mL finely chopped fresh parsley 2 tbsp./30 mL drained capers	*Add basil, parsley and capers to skillet and stir in.*
salt *(to taste)* freshly ground black pepper *(to taste)*	*Season with salt and pepper.*
2 tbsp./30 mL finely chopped fresh parsley	*Spoon contents of skillet over halibut steaks on platter. Sprinkle with parsley and serve immediately. Serve directly from platter to individual plates.*

PAN-FRIED HALIBUT STEAK
WITH RED, GREEN AND YELLOW PEPPERS
AND BALSAMIC VINEGAR
Serves 4
Bistecca d' Ippoglosso Tre Colore

4 (6-8 oz./175-250 g) fresh halibut steaks
salt *(to taste)*
freshly ground black pepper *(to taste)*
dash of onion powder
flour *(to dust)*

Rinse halibut steaks under cold running water and pat dry with paper towels. Season with salt, pepper and onion powder. Dust with flour.

1/4 cup/50 mL vegetable oil
2 tbsp./30 mL butter

Fry halibut steaks in oil and butter in a skillet for 4-5 minutes per side until golden brown, then remove from skillet and put on a platter. Remove skin and centre bone from steaks, if desired, and discard. Set platter aside and keep warm.

1/2 medium red pepper, seeded and julienned
1/2 medium green pepper, seeded and julienned
1/2 medium yellow pepper, seeded and julienned
3 tbsp./45 mL olive oil

Sauté red, green and yellow peppers in olive oil in a skillet for 1-2 minutes. Be careful not to burn the peppers.

2 tbsp./30 mL balsamic vinegar
juice of 1/2 lemon
2 tbsp./30 mL extra virgin olive oil
2 tbsp./30 mL butter

Add balsamic vinegar, lemon juice, olive oil and butter to skillet and simmer for approximately 1 minute.

salt *(to taste)*
freshly ground black pepper *(to taste)*

Season with salt and pepper.

1 tbsp./15 mL finely chopped fresh parsley

Spoon contents of skillet over halibut steaks on platter. Sprinkle with parsley and serve immediately. Serve directly from platter to individual plates.

PAN-FRIED HALIBUT STEAK
WITH TUNA SAUCE
Bistecca d' Ippoglosso con Salsa Tonnata

Serves 4

4 (6-8 oz./175-250 g) fresh halibut steaks
salt *(to taste)*
freshly ground black pepper *(to taste)*
juice of 1/2 lemon
flour *(to dust)*

Rinse halibut steaks under cold running water and pat dry with paper towels. Season with salt and pepper. Sprinkle with lemon juice. Dust with flour.

1/4 cup/50 mL olive oil
2 tbsp./30 mL butter

Fry halibut steaks in oil and butter in a skillet for 4-5 minutes per side until golden brown, then remove from skillet and put on a platter. Remove skin and centre bone from steaks, if desired, and discard. Set platter aside and keep warm.

1 (6 1/2 oz./184 g) tin of chunk light tuna, packed in oil — do not drain *(tuna must be packed in oil)*
1/2 cup/125 mL chicken stock *(see p. 7)*
3 tbsp./45 mL mayonnaise *(see p. 14)*
3 tbsp./45 mL olive oil
juice of 1/2 lemon

Put contents of tin of tuna, chicken stock, mayonnaise, olive oil and lemon juice in a blender and process until smooth, then transfer contents of blender to a bowl.

2 tbsp./30 mL drained capers

Add capers to bowl and stir in.

salt *(to taste)*
freshly ground black pepper *(to taste)*

Season with salt and pepper.

1 tbsp./15 mL finely chopped fresh parsley

Spoon contents of bowl over halibut steaks on platter. Sprinkle with parsley and serve immediately. Serve directly from platter to individual plates.

SAUTEED HALIBUT STEAK
WITH RHUBARB
Bistecca d' Ippoglosso con Rabarbaro

Serves 4

4 (6-8 oz./175-250 g) fresh halibut steaks
salt *(to taste)*
white pepper *(to taste)*
juice of 1 lemon
4-6 drops of Worcestershire sauce
flour *(to dust)*

Rinse halibut steaks under cold running water and pat dry with paper towels. Season with salt and pepper. Sprinkle with lemon juice and Worcestershire sauce. Dust with flour.

1/3 cup/75 mL vegetable oil
2 tbsp./30 mL butter

Sauté halibut steaks in oil and butter in a skillet for 3-4 minutes per side until golden brown, then remove from skillet and put on a platter. Remove skin and centre bone from steaks, if desired, and discard. Set platter aside and keep warm.

4 tbsp./60 mL brunoise of rhubarb — rhubarb diced very fine and cooked in ingredients below
2 tbsp./30 mL dry white wine
juice of 1 lemon
1/4 tsp./1 mL sugar

Sauté rhubarb in white wine, lemon juice and sugar in a saucepan for approximately 1 minute.

5 tbsp./75 mL butter

Add butter to saucepan and blend in.

1 1/2 tbsp./20 mL finely chopped fresh mint

Add mint to saucepan and stir in.

salt *(to taste)*
white pepper *(to taste)*

Season with salt and pepper.

Spoon contents of saucepan over halibut steaks on platter and serve immediately. Serve directly from platter to individual plates.

MACKEREL
Sgombro

Background: *Mackerel are found all over the world and are available, fresh and frozen, all year round. Their flesh, which is a light reddish colour, is highly perishable and should be consumed right away. If it is not consumed right away, it will pick up a bitter taste. Mackerel are an attractive fish, with silver blue upper surfaces, silvery iridescent sides and silvery-white bellies. They range in weight from 1/2-2 lbs./250 g-1 kg and are usually sold whole or in fillets. In the European market, they are known canned. Mackerel are high in fat content and are generally considered an oily fish.*

BAKED WHOLE MACKEREL
WITH VEGETABLES
Sgombro con Salsa Rustica

Serves 4

4 (12-16 oz./350-500 g) whole fresh mackerel, cleaned and boned
salt *(to taste)*
freshly ground black pepper *(to taste)*
flour *(to coat)*

Rinse mackerel under cold running water and pat dry with paper towels. Season with salt and pepper. Dredge in flour.

1/4 cup/50 mL vegetable oil
2 tbsp./30 mL butter

Fry opened mackerel in oil and butter in a skillet for approximately 2 minutes per side until golden brown, then remove from skillet and lay fish open, skin side down, in a buttered baking dish. Set aside.

Pre-heat oven to 350°F/180°C.

4 firm, ripe tomatoes, eyes removed and scored "x" on top

Blanch tomatoes in a pot of rapidly boiling water for 20 seconds, then plunge into a pot of cold water to stop the cooking. Peel, seed and chop tomatoes.

Cover fish with tomatoes.

2 stalks of celery, washed, threaded and chopped
1/2 cup/125 mL washed and chopped leeks — use only the white part
2 cups/500 mL cleaned, whole small fresh mushrooms
1 clove of garlic, peeled and crushed

Cover tomatoes with celery, leeks, mushrooms and garlic.

(cont'd over)

salt *(to taste)*
freshly ground black pepper *(to taste)*

Season with salt and pepper.

1/3 cup/75 mL dry white wine

Add white wine to baking dish.

4 tbsp./60 mL fresh fine white breadcrumbs
4 tbsp./60 mL freshly grated Parmesan cheese

Sprinkle vegetables with breadcrumbs and Parmesan cheese.

Put baking dish in oven and bake for 18-22 minutes until fish is done.

Remove baking dish from oven and put mackerel, with vegetables on top, on a platter. Serve immediately. Serve directly from platter to individual plates.

GRILLED WHOLE MACKEREL
WITH TOMATO CHILI SALSA
Sgombro Grigliato Piccante

Serves 4

4 (12-16 oz./350-500 g) whole fresh
mackerel, cleaned and boned
salt *(to taste)*
freshly ground black pepper *(to taste)*
juice of 1 lemon
1 tsp./5 mL peeled and
finely chopped garlic
olive oil *(to coat)*

Rinse mackerel under cold running water and pat dry with paper towels. Lightly score outside of fish. Season with salt and pepper. Sprinkle with lemon juice and garlic. Rub with olive oil.

1 lemon, cut in half

Put opened mackerel on the oiled rack of a barbecue and cook over hot coals for approximately 5 minutes per side, squeezing with lemon juice, until fish is done.

1 tbsp./15 mL extra virgin olive oil
juice of 1/2 lemon
1 cup/250 mL tomato chili salsa
(see below)

When fish is done, remove from barbecue and lay open, skin side down, on a platter. Sprinkle with olive oil and lemon juice and serve immediately. Serve directly from platter to individual plates. Serve with tomato chili salsa in a bowl on the side.

Tomato Chili Salsa:

Makes 3 cups/750 mL

1/2 medium onion,
peeled and finely chopped
3 tbsp./45 mL olive oil

Sauté onion in oil in a skillet for 2-3 minutes until soft and transparent.

1/4 tsp./1 mL peeled and
finely chopped garlic

Add garlic to skillet and sauté for approximately 1 minute.

3 cups/750 mL tomato sauce
(see p. 11)
1 small Jalapeño green pepper,
seeded and finely chopped

Add tomato sauce and green pepper to skillet and bring to a boil. Reduce heat and simmer for 3-5 minutes.

2 tbsp./30 mL extra virgin olive oil

Add olive oil to skillet and blend in.

salt *(to taste)*
freshly ground black pepper *(to taste)*

Season with salt and pepper.

Put 1 cup/250 mL tomato chili salsa in a bowl and serve with grilled mackerel.

Leftover tomato chili salsa may be stored in a sealed plastic container in the refrigerator for approximately 1 week.

MAHI MAHI
Mahi Mahi

Background: *Mahi mahi is a member of the dolphin family. They are found only in tropical oceans of the world, most notably around Hawaii. Mahi mahi range in weight from 12-36 lbs./6-18 kg and have moderate fat content. They have firm, flavourful flesh and are available all year round. The catch of mahi mahi is small when compared to the demand, so mahi mahi is not widely available beyond its locale.*

PAN-FRIED MAHI MAHI
COATED IN MACADAMIA NUTS
Mahi Mahi in Padella con Salsa Havaiana

Serves 4

4 (6-8 oz./175-250 g) fillets of fresh mahi mahi
salt *(to taste)*
freshly ground black pepper *(to taste)*
juice of 1 lime
2 tbsp./30 mL milk
2 drops of Worcestershire sauce
1 cup/250 mL ground macadamia nuts *(to coat)*

Rinse fillets of mahi mahi under cold running water and pat dry with paper towels. Season with salt and pepper. Sprinkle with lime juice, Worcestershire sauce and milk. Dredge in macadamia nuts. Press macadamia nuts onto mahi mahi.

1/4 cup/50 mL peanut oil
2 tbsp./30 mL butter

Fry mahi mahi in oil and butter in a skillet for 5-7 minutes per side until golden brown, then remove from skillet, put on a platter, set aside and keep warm.

5 tbsp./75 mL butter

Melt butter in a saucepan.

juice of 1 lime
2 drops of Worcestershire sauce

Add lime juice and Worcestershire sauce to saucepan and blend in.

3 tbsp./45 mL chopped macadamia nuts
1 tbsp./15 mL finely chopped fresh parsley

Add macadamia nuts and parsley to saucepan and toss to coat with butter.

salt *(to taste)*
freshly ground black pepper *(to taste)*

Season with salt and pepper.

Spoon contents of saucepan over fillets of mahi mahi on platter and serve immediately. Serve directly from platter to individual plates.

GRILLED MAHI MAHI
MARINATED IN PINEAPPLE JUICE
Mahi Mahi alla Griglia con Sugo d' Ananas

Serves 4

4 (6-8 oz./175-250 g) fillets of fresh mahi mahi	*Rinse fillets of mahi mahi under cold running water and pat dry with paper towels.*
1/2 cup/125 mL pineapple juice juice of 1 lime 4 tbsp./60 mL vegetable oil dash of cayenne	*Put pineapple juice, lime juice, vegetable oil and cayenne in a baking dish and mix together.*
	Marinate mahi mahi in pineapple juice mixture in baking dish in the refrigerator for 20-40 minutes, then remove dish from refrigerator. Drain mahi mahi and reserve marinade for basting while mahi mahi is barbecuing.
salt *(to taste)* freshly ground black pepper *(to taste)* 1/2 tsp./2 mL peeled and finely chopped garlic peanut oil *(to coat)*	*Season mahi mahi with salt and pepper. Sprinkle with garlic and rub with peanut oil.*
4 slices of fresh pineapple — rind removed vegetable oil *(to coat pineapple)*	*Put mahi mahi on the oiled rack of a barbecue and cook over hot coals for 5-7 minutes per side, basting with marinade and turning to trellis-mark, until fish is done. Near the end of 5-7 minutes cooking time, grill pineapple slices that have been brushed with vegetable oil on the barbecue until they are hot.*
1 lime, cut into 4 wedges	*When fish is done, remove from barbecue and put on a platter or individual plates. Top each fillet with 1 slice of cooked pineapple and garnish platter or plates with lime wedges. Serve immediately.*

MONKFISH
Rospo di Mare

Background: *Monkfish are an odd-looking Atlantic ocean fish, also known as angler, goosefish and lotte. They are easily identifiable by their large spiny heads and wide mouths with fang-like teeth. Other names for monkfish have included: all-mouth, abbotfish, fishing frog, rapefish, sea devil, diable de mer, poisson-pêcheur and bellyfish. Only their tails are marketed. Monkfish range greatly in weight, from 2-50 lbs./1-25 kg, and are available fresh from June to September. They are low in fat content and have firm, dense flesh, with a mild, sweet flavour. Their flavour comes from their diet, which is, most notably, shellfish. For many years, monkfish was considered uninteresting, but it is a fish that is gaining popularity in the marketplace.*

BAKED FILLET OF MONKFISH SERVED ON A BED OF RADICCHIO WITH ZUCCHINI CREAM SAUCE
Rospo di Mare al Forno con Radicchio

Serves 4

1 1/2 lbs./700 g fillets of fresh monkfish — cut into 12 (2 oz./50 g) portions
salt *(to taste)*
white pepper *(to taste)*
1/8 tsp./pinch of finely chopped fresh oregano
flour *(to dust)*

Rinse monkfish under cold running water and pat dry with paper towels. Season with salt, pepper and oregano. Dust with flour. Set aside.

1 head of radicchio, washed, dried and julienned

Make a bed of radicchio in a buttered baking pan and set aside.

1/4 cup/50 mL olive oil

Sear monkfish in hot oil in a skillet, then remove from skillet and put on top of radicchio in baking pan.

Pre-heat oven to 375°F/190°C.

1/4 cup/50 mL chicken stock *(see p. 7)*

Add chicken stock to baking pan.

Put baking pan in oven and bake for 12-15 minutes until fish is done.

1 medium zucchini,
washed and chopped
1 tbsp./15 mL peeled and
finely chopped shallots
1 tsp./5 mL peeled and
finely chopped garlic
3 tbsp./45 mL olive oil

While monkfish is baking in oven, sauté zucchini, shallots and garlic in a skillet for 4-5 minutes until zucchini is tender, then transfer contents of skillet to a blender and purée. Return zucchini purée to skillet and heat.

1/2 cup/125 mL whipping cream

Add cream to skillet and blend in.

2 tbsp./30 mL butter

Add butter to skillet and blend in.

juice of 1/2 lemon

Add lemon juice to skillet and blend in.

salt *(to taste)*
white pepper *(to taste)*

Season with salt and pepper.

4 tbsp./60 mL brunoise of zucchini
— zucchini diced very fine
and cooked in butter

When monkfish has finished baking, remove baking pan from oven and put monkfish, on top of radicchio, on a platter. Spoon zucchini sauce in skillet over monkfish and radicchio on platter. Garnish with a brunoise of zucchini and serve immediately. Serve directly from platter to individual plates.

GRILLED FILLET OF MONKFISH MARINATED IN ORANGE JUICE AND TARRAGON
Serves 4

Rospo di Mare alla Griglia con Arancia e Dragoncello

1 1/2 lbs./700 g fillets of fresh monkfish — cut into 12 (2 oz./50 g) portions	*Rinse monkfish under cold running water and pat dry with paper towels.*
1 1/2 cups/375 mL freshly squeezed orange juice — reserving 1/2 cup/ 125 mL orange juice for sauce 2 tbsp./30 mL peanut oil 2 tbsp./30 mL finely chopped fresh tarragon	*Put orange juice, peanut oil and tarragon in a baking dish and mix together.*
	Marinate monkfish in orange juice mixture in baking dish in the refrigerator for 1 hour, then remove dish from refrigerator. Drain monkfish and reserve marinade for basting while monkfish is barbecuing.
salt *(to taste)* freshly ground black pepper *(to taste)* peanut oil *(to coat)*	*Season monkfish with salt and pepper and rub with peanut oil.*
	Put monkfish on the oiled rack of a barbecue and cook over hot coals for 2-3 minutes per side, basting with marinade, until fish is done.
	When fish is done, remove from barbecue, put on a platter, set aside and keep warm.
1/2 cup/125 mL freshly squeezed orange juice *(reserved above)* 2 tbsp./30 mL dry white wine 1 tbsp./15 mL tarragon vinegar 1 tsp./5 mL peeled and finely chopped shallots	*Put orange juice, white wine, tarragon vinegar and shallots in a saucepan and simmer until liquid has reduced by one-half.*
2 tbsp./30 mL butter	*Add butter to saucepan and blend in.*
salt *(to taste)* freshly ground black pepper *(to taste)* 1 tbsp./15 mL finely chopped fresh tarragon	*Season with salt, pepper and tarragon.*

6 sections of fresh orange, peeled, seeded and halved

Spoon contents of saucepan over monkfish on platter. Garnish each fillet of monkfish with 1 half section of orange and serve immediately. Serve directly from platter to individual plates.

MONKFISH SCHNITZEL
Cotoletta di Rospo di Mare

Serves 4

1 1/2 lbs./700 g fillets of fresh monkfish — cut into 12 (2 oz./50 g) portions
salt *(to taste)*
white pepper *(to taste)*
flour *(to coat)*

Rinse monkfish under cold running water and pat dry with paper towels. Gently pound fillets between 2 sheets of plastic wrap until they are 1/4 inch//6 mm thick. Season with salt and pepper, then dredge in flour, shaking off the excess.

2 eggs, beaten
1 tbsp./15 mL milk

Mix eggs and milk together in a bowl.

salt *(to taste)*
white pepper *(to taste)*
1/8 tsp./pinch of ground nutmeg

Season with salt, pepper and nutmeg.

fresh fine white breadcrumbs *(to coat)*

Dip monkfish in egg mixture, then roll in breadcrumbs. Press breadcrumbs onto monkfish.

1/2 cup/125 mL peanut oil

Fry monkfish in oil in a skillet for 3-5 minutes per side until golden brown, then remove from skillet, put on a platter, set aside and keep warm.

4 tbsp./60 mL butter

Melt butter in a saucepan.

juice of 1/2 lemon

Add lemon juice to saucepan and blend in.

2 tbsp./30 mL drained capers
1 tbsp./15 mL finely chopped fresh parsley

Add capers and parsley to saucepan and heat.

salt *(to taste)*
freshly ground black pepper *(to taste)*

Season with salt and pepper.

Spoon contents of saucepan over monkfish on platter and serve immediately. Serve directly from platter to individual plates.

OCEAN PERCH
Pesce Persico

Background: *Pacific ocean perch are rockfish; Atlantic ocean perch are redfish. Pacific ocean perch are bright red, with olive stippling on their sides, and they have projecting lower jaws. They range in weight from 1-3 lbs./500 g-1.5 kg and are low in fat content. They are available fresh all year round and are sold, for the most part, as fillets. Atlantic ocean perch is also known as: bream, sea bream, Norway haddock, rosefish and red perch. They are small spiny fish and weigh only approximately 1 lb./500 g. They have black eyes and orange to flame-red bodies. They are caught nearshore and offshore in April, then again from June to October. They have medium fat content and are available whole or in fillets.*

BAKED FILLET OF OCEAN PERCH
WITH SOUR CREAM AND DILL
Filetti di Pesce Persico al Forno in Agrodolce

Serves 4

4 (6-8 oz./175-250 g) fillets of fresh ocean perch
salt *(to taste)*
freshly ground black pepper *(to taste)*

Rinse fillets of ocean perch under cold running water and pat dry with paper towels. Season with salt and pepper.

1/4 cup/50 mL vegetable oil
2 tbsp./30 mL butter

Sear ocean perch in hot oil and butter in a skillet for 1-2 minutes per side, then remove from skillet and put in a buttered baking dish.

Pre-heat oven to 400°F/200°C.

1 cup/250 mL sour cream
3 tbsp./45 mL Dijon mustard
3 tbsp./45 mL finely chopped fresh dill

Mix sour cream, mustard and dill together in a bowl.

salt *(to taste)*
white pepper *(to taste)*

Season with salt and pepper.

Spread sour cream mixture over top of fillets of ocean perch in baking dish.

Put baking dish in oven and bake for 12-15 minutes until fish is done.

2 tbsp./30 mL finely chopped fresh dill

Transfer contents of baking dish to a platter. Sprinkle with dill and serve immediately. Serve directly from platter to individual plates.

GRILLED FILLET OF OCEAN PERCH
WITH ROSEMARY AND LEMON HALVES *Serves 4*
Filetti di Pesce Persico al Rosmarino

4 (6-8 oz./175-250 g) fillets of fresh
ocean perch
salt *(to taste)*
freshly ground black pepper *(to taste)*
juice of 1 lemon
1 1/2 tbsp./20 mL chopped
fresh rosemary
4 tbsp./60 mL extra virgin olive oil

1 lemon, cut in half

Rinse fillets of ocean perch under cold running water and pat dry with paper towels. Season with salt and pepper and put in a baking dish. Sprinkle with rosemary and drizzle with 1 tbsp./ 15 mL olive oil per fillet. Put baking dish in the refrigerator for 20 minutes, then remove dish from refrigerator.

Put ocean perch on the oiled rack of a barbecue and cook over hot coals for 6-8 minutes per side, squeezing with lemon juice, until fish is done.

4 small sprigs of fresh rosemary
2 lemons, cut in half

When fish is done, remove from barbecue and put on a platter or individual plates. Garnish each fillet of ocean perch with 1 sprig of rosemary. Garnish platter or plates with lemon halves and serve immediately.

PAN-FRIED FILLET OF OCEAN PERCH
WITH EGGPLANT AND OLIVES
Filetti di Pesce Persico Siciliana

Serves 4

4 (6-8 oz./175-250 g) fillets of fresh ocean perch	*Rinse fillets of ocean perch under cold running water and pat dry with paper towels. Set aside.*
1 eggplant, top removed and cut into 2 x 1 inch/5 x 1 cm pieces salt *(to taste)*	*Put pieces of eggplant on a paper towel on a tray and sprinkle with salt. Let eggplant stand for 20 minutes, then rinse under cold running water, drain and set aside.*
salt *(to taste)* freshly ground black pepper *(to taste)* dash of onion salt flour *(to dust)*	*Season ocean perch with salt, pepper and onion salt. Dust with flour.*
1/4 cup/50 mL olive oil	*Fry ocean perch in oil in a skillet for 5-6 minutes per side until golden brown, then remove from skillet, put on a platter, set aside and keep warm.*
1/4 cup/50 mL olive oil	*Replenish oil in skillet.*
	Add eggplant to skillet and sauté for approximately 3 minutes.
2 cups/500 mL tomato sauce *(see p. 11)*	*Add tomato sauce to skillet and bring to a boil. Reduce heat and simmer for approximately 3 minutes.*
8-12 Calamata black olives, pitted and sliced	*Add olives to skillet and heat to warm.*
salt *(to taste)* freshly ground black pepper *(to taste)* 1/8 tsp./pinch of seeded and finely chopped hot red chili pepper	*Season with salt, pepper and chili pepper.*
2 tbsp./30 mL extra virgin olive oil 1 tbsp./15 mL finely chopped fresh flat-leaved Italian parsley	*Spoon contents of skillet over fillets of ocean perch on platter. Drizzle with olive oil. Sprinkle with parsley and serve immediately. Serve directly from platter to individual plates.*

ORANGE ROUGHY
Orange Roughy

Background: *Orange roughy, also known as deep sea perch, are imported from New Zealand, where they are fished off the South Island. They are caught by trawling and are available from May to July, then again from October to February. They weigh an average of 3 lbs./1.5 kg. They have medium firm-textured, pearly-white flesh, which flakes coarsely when cooked, and a delicate shellfish flavour, which makes them quite desirable. They are sold as fillets. Orange roughy is a relatively new fish in the marketplace, but it is a fish that is winning praise and gaining a following.*

GRILLED FILLET OF ORANGE ROUGHY WITH ROSEMARY SAUCE
Serves 4
Orange Roughy alla Griglia con Rosmarino

4 (6 oz./175 g) fillets of fresh orange roughy
salt *(to taste)*
freshly ground black pepper *(to taste)*
juice of 1 lemon
2 tbsp./30 mL chopped fresh rosemary
1/4 cup/50 mL extra virgin olive oil

Rinse fillets of orange roughy under cold running water and pat dry with paper towels. Season with salt and pepper and put in a baking dish. Sprinkle with lemon juice and rosemary. Drizzle with olive oil. Put baking dish in the refrigerator for 20 minutes, then remove dish from refrigerator.

Put orange roughy on the oiled rack of a barbecue and cook over hot coals for approximately 6 minutes per side until fish is done.

4 sprigs of fresh rosemary
1 lemon, cut into 4 wedges
rosemary sauce *(see below)*

When fish is done, remove from barbecue and put on a platter. Garnish each fillet with 1 sprig of rosemary. Garnish platter with lemon wedges and serve immediately. Serve directly from platter to individual plates. Serve with rosemary sauce in a sauceboat on the side.

Rosemary Sauce:

1 1/2 tbsp./20 mL chopped fresh rosemary
1 tsp./5 mL peeled and finely chopped shallots
1/2 cup/125 mL dry white wine

Simmer rosemary and shallots in white wine in a saucepan until wine has reduced by two-thirds.

(cont'd over)

2 tbsp./30 mL whipping cream	*Add cream to saucepan and blend in. Simmer for approximately 1 minute, then remove saucepan from heat.*
4 tbsp./60 mL butter	*Add butter to saucepan and blend in.*
juice of 1/2 lemon	*Add lemon juice to saucepan and blend in.*
salt *(to taste)* white pepper *(to taste)*	*Season with salt and pepper.*
	Transfer contents of saucepan to a sauceboat and serve warm.

PAN-FRIED FILLET OF ORANGE ROUGHY
WITH LIME-CHIVE BUTTER
Serves 4
Orange Roughy Saltato con Burro di Cedro

4 (6 oz./175 g) fillets of fresh orange roughy salt *(to taste)* white pepper *(to taste)* juice of 1 lemon dash of Worcestershire sauce flour *(to dust)*	*Rinse fillets of orange roughy under cold running water and pat dry with paper towels. Season with salt and pepper. Sprinkle with lemon juice and Worcestershire sauce. Dust with flour.*
2 tbsp./30 mL vegetable oil 2 tbsp./30 mL butter	*Fry orange roughy in oil and butter in a skillet for 4-5 minutes per side, then remove from skillet and put on a platter or individual plates. Serve immediately.*
lime-chive butter *(see below)*	*Serve with lime-chive butter in a sauceboat on the side.*

Lime-Chive Butter:

1 tbsp./15 mL peeled and finely chopped shallots 2 tbsp./30 mL dry white wine juice of 1 lime	*Sauté shallots in white wine and lime juice in a saucepan for approximately 1 minute.*
5-6 tbsp./75-90 mL butter	*Add butter to saucepan and blend in.*
2 tbsp./30 mL chopped fresh chives	*Add chives to saucepan and stir in.*
salt *(to taste)* white pepper *(to taste)*	*Season with salt and pepper.*
	Transfer contents of saucepan to a sauceboat and serve warm.

RED SNAPPER
Scorfano

Background: *True red snapper is found in the Gulf of Mexico, the Caribbean and in the Pacific ocean, off the coast of Mexico. True snapper are vivid rose pink, fading to pink, and have bright red eyes. They range in weight from 2-30 lbs./1-15 kg and are low in fat content. They are available all year round and come whole or in fillets. Pacific red snapper, which is widely available on the Pacific coast, is actually yelloweye rockfish, a member of the rockfish family, and should not be confused with true red snapper. Pacific red snapper are red-orange, washed with pink on their backs and sides, becoming paler underneath, and they have yellow eyes. They weigh up to 10 lbs./5 kg and are low in fat content. They are available all year round and come whole or in fillets. Red snapper, whether it be true or Pacific, is an extremely popular fish. It is adaptable to any cooking method.*

BAKED WHOLE RED SNAPPER
Scorfano Intero al Forno

Serves 4

1 (4-6 lb./2-3 kg) whole fresh red snapper, scaled — with the fins and gills removed

Rinse red snapper under cold running water and pat dry with paper towels. Set aside.

3 tbsp./45 mL peeled and finely chopped onion
1 large stalk of celery, washed, threaded and finely chopped
3 tbsp./45 mL butter

Sauté onion and celery in butter in a skillet for 2-3 minutes until onion is soft and transparent, then transfer contents of skillet to a bowl.

3-4 cups/750 mL-1 L day-old white breadcubes — 1/2 inch/1 cm cubes

Add breadcubes to bowl and mix together.

1 large egg
3/4 cup/175 mL sour cream
1 tsp./5 mL lemon zest
2 tbsp./30 mL finely chopped fresh parsley
1 tbsp./15 mL chopped fresh chives

Add egg, sour cream, lemon zest, parsley and chives to bowl and mix together.

1/2 cup/125 mL fresh shrimp — or 1/2 cup/125 mL fresh crabmeat (or 1/4 cup/50 mL of each)

Add shrimp or crabmeat to bowl and gently mix together.

salt *(to taste)*
white pepper *(to taste)*

Season with salt and pepper.

Pre-heat oven to 350°F/180°C.

(cont'd over)

salt *(to taste)* white pepper *(to taste)* 1/8 tsp./pinch of paprika juice of 1 lemon 1 clove of garlic, peeled and crushed 2 tbsp./30 mL melted butter	*Season red snapper, inside and out, with salt, pepper and paprika. Sprinkle with lemon juice. Rub with garlic and drizzle with butter.*
	Stuff cavity of fish with breadcube stuffing and put red snapper on a buttered baking tray.
juice of 1 lemon 1-2 tbsp./15-30 mL melted butter	*Put baking tray in oven and bake for 45-60 minutes, basting with lemon juice and butter, until fish is done.*
sprigs of fresh parsley 2 lemons, cut into 8 wedges	*When fish is done, remove baking tray from oven and put red snapper on a platter. Garnish platter with sprigs of parsley and lemon wedges. Serve immediately. Cut into slices at the table. Serve directly from platter to individual plates.*

BROILED FILLET OF RED SNAPPER
Filetti di Scorfano in Graticola

Serves 4

Pre-heat oven to broil/grill.

4 (6-8 oz./175-250 g) fillets of fresh
red snapper
salt *(to taste)*
freshly ground black pepper *(to taste)*
juice of 1/2 lemon or lime
4 drops of Worcestershire sauce
1/8 tsp./pinch of finely chopped
fresh oregano
6 tbsp./90 mL freshly grated
Parmesan cheese
4 tsp./20 mL melted butter

Rinse fillets of red snapper under cold running water and pat dry with paper towels. Season with salt and pepper and put on a buttered baking tray. Sprinkle with lemon or lime juice, Worcestershire sauce and oregano, then sprinkle each fillet with 1 1/2 tbsp./20 mL Parmesan cheese and drizzle with 1 tsp./5 mL butter per fillet.

Put baking tray in oven and broil/grill for 10-15 minutes until golden brown.

Remove tray from oven. Put fillets of red snapper on a platter or individual plates and serve immediately.

GRILLED FILLET OF RED SNAPPER
MARINATED IN OLIVE OIL AND GARLIC
Scorfano ai Ferri Salsa Olio e Aglio

Serves 4

4 (6-8 oz./175-250 g) fillets of fresh
red snapper
salt *(to taste)*
freshly ground black pepper *(to taste)*
1 tbsp./15 mL peeled and
finely chopped garlic
4 tbsp./60 mL extra virgin olive oil
juice of 1/2 lemon

Rinse fillets of red snapper under cold running water and pat dry with paper towels. Season with salt and pepper and put in a baking dish. Sprinkle with garlic and drizzle with olive oil. Put baking dish in the refrigerator for 1 hour, then remove dish from refrigerator and sprinkle fillets with lemon juice.

1 lemon, cut in half

Put red snapper on the oiled rack of a barbecue and cook over hot coals for 5-7 minutes per side, squeezing with lemon juice, until fish is done.

4 tsp./20 mL extra virgin olive oil
1 lemon, cut into 4 wedges

When fish is done, remove from barbecue and put on a platter or individual plates. Drizzle each fillet of red snapper with 1 tsp./5 mL olive oil. Garnish platter or plates with lemon wedges and serve immediately.

RED SNAPPER CASSEROLE
Filetti di Scorfano in Casseruola

Serves 4

1 1/2 lbs./700 g fillet of fresh
red snapper — cut into 2 inch/
5 cm cubes
8 cups/2 L cold water
1 tbsp./15 mL salt
2 tbsp./30 mL white vinegar

*Blanch cubes of red snapper in a
pot of rapidly boiling salted water
to which vinegar has been added
for 1-2 minutes to firm up fish,
then drain pot and let red snapper
stand while preparing vegetables.*

1 medium onion, peeled
and diced in 1/2 inch/1 cm cubes
1/2 lb./250 g okra,
sliced into 1/2 inch/1 cm pieces
1/4 cup/50 mL olive oil

*Sauté onion and okra in oil in a
pot for approximately 3 minutes.*

2 stalks of celery, washed, threaded
and diced in 1/2 inch/1 cm pieces
1 small red pepper, seeded
and cut into 1/2 inch/1 cm squares
1 small green pepper, seeded
and cut into 1/2 inch/1 cm squares

*Add celery and red and green peppers
to pot and sauté for approximately
3 minutes.*

1 (28 oz./796 mL) can of peeled
Italian plum tomatoes
— and tomato liquid
2 peeled, seeded and chopped
fresh tomatoes
1 tsp./5 mL peeled and
finely chopped garlic
2 tbsp./30 mL finely chopped
fresh parsley

*Add tomatoes and tomato liquid,
fresh tomatoes, garlic and parsley to pot
and bring to a boil. Reduce heat and
simmer for 3-5 minutes.*

Add red snapper to pot.

salt *(to taste)*
freshly ground black pepper *(to taste)*
1/2 tsp./2 mL finely chopped
fresh oregano

*Season with salt, pepper and oregano.
Set aside.*

Pre-heat oven to 350°F/180°C.

4 slices of fresh white bread,
crusts removed and cut into
2 inch/5 cm squares
1/2 cup/125 mL milk

*Soak bread in milk in a bowl,
then squeeze dry.*

*Add bread to pot with red snapper and
vegetables and gently mix together.*

1 cup/250 mL fresh fine white
breadcrumbs
2 tbsp./30 mL freshly grated
Parmesan cheese

*Transfer contents of pot to a
buttered casserole dish. Sprinkle with
breadcrumbs and Parmesan cheese.*

Put casserole dish in oven and bake for 15-20 minutes, then remove dish from oven and serve immediately. Serve directly from casserole dish to individual plates.

SAUTEED CUBED FILLET OF RED SNAPPER WITH RED AND YELLOW PEPPERS AND GREEN AND BLACK OLIVES
Filetti di Scorfano con Peperone Rosso-Giallo e Olive Verde-Nero

Serves 4

1 1/2 lbs./700 g fillet of fresh red snapper — cut into 2 inch/ 5 cm cubes
salt *(to taste)*
white pepper *(to taste)*
juice of 1/2 lemon
flour *(to dust)*

Rinse cubes of red snapper under cold running water and pat dry with paper towels. Season with salt and pepper. Sprinkle with lemon juice. Dust with flour.

1/4 cup/50 mL vegetable oil
2 tbsp./30 mL olive oil

Sauté red snapper in oil in a skillet for 2-3 minutes.

1 red pepper, seeded and cut into 1 inch/2 cm squares
1 yellow pepper, seeded and cut into 1 inch/2 cm squares
1 tsp./5 mL peeled and finely chopped garlic

Add red and yellow peppers and garlic to skillet and sauté for approximately 2 minutes.

3 tbsp./45 mL dry white wine or vermouth
juice of 1/2 lemon

Add white wine or vermouth and lemon juice to skillet and simmer for approximately 2 minutes.

3 tbsp./45 mL butter

Add butter to skillet and blend in.

8 Calamata black olives, pitted and halved
8 Calamata green olives, pitted and halved

Add olives to skillet and heat to warm.

salt *(to taste)*
white pepper *(to taste)*

Season with salt and pepper.

1 tbsp./15 mL finely chopped fresh parsley
2 1/2 cups/625 mL cooked long grain white rice *(to accompany)*

Transfer contents of skillet to a a platter or individual plates. Sprinkle with parsley and serve immediately. Serve with rice.

SALMON
Salmone

Background: *Pacific salmon come in five species, of which the chinook or spring salmon is the largest. Chinook or spring salmon are silver on their sides and dark green to black on their backs, with numerous small black spots on their tails fins. They range in weight from 8-44 lbs./4-22 kg and are also known as king salmon. They are caught first in the season and are available from April to September. They are thought to be the most flavourful of Pacific salmon because they spend the longest amount of time in the ocean and they travel the farthest upriver to spawn. Also available is the coho or silver salmon, so named because of their colouring, with silver on their sides and metallic blue to green on their backs. Coho or silver salmon range in weight from 4-10 lbs./2-5 kg and are available fresh from July to October. They migrate only a short distance upstream to spawn. The third species available, with the brightest-coloured flesh, is the sockeye salmon, commonly called Pacific salmon or red salmon. They are a favourite for canning. Sockeye salmon are silver on their sides, shading to greenish blue on their backs. Their average weight is 6 lbs./3 kg. They are netted off the mouths of rivers and they are available fresh from June to September, but, most notably, in July. Sockeye salmon are highly prized in foreign markets, such as Japan and Europe, because of the colour of their flesh. The fourth species available is the pink salmon, which are the smallest species. They range in weight from 3-5 lbs./1.5-2.5 kg and are available fresh from July to September. They are silver on their sides and dark blue on their backs and can be distinguished easily by large oval-shaped spots on their tail fins. The fifth species available is the chum or keta salmon. They are similar to sockeye salmon in appearance, but they have a narrower wrist at their tail. They are silver on their sides, shading to metallic dark blue on their backs. They range in weight from 7-14 lbs./3.5-7 kg and are available fresh from July to November. There is great debate as to whether Pacific or Atlantic salmon is better tasting. Opinion varies and is extremely chauvinistic, but it tends to favour Atlantic salmon, of which there is only one species. Atlantic salmon are harvested inshore and nearshore and are available fresh from May through August. They are silver on their sides and bellies, with their upper parts ranging through various shades of brown, blue and green, and they have an average weight of 9 lbs./4.5 kg. Salmon is perhaps the oldest known gourmet food in the world and each country that has salmon claims theirs to be the best. Salmon are high in fat content and are adaptable to any cooking method.*

BAKED STUFFED BABY SALMON
Serves 4
Salmone Ripieno alla Ghiotta

4 (8-10 oz./250-300 g) whole fresh baby salmon, cleaned and boned — with the heads and tails left on	*Rinse each salmon under cold running water and pat dry with paper towels. Set aside.*
3 tbsp./45 mL peeled and finely chopped onion 1 large stalk of celery, washed, threaded and finely chopped 3 tbsp./45 mL butter	*Sauté onion and celery in butter in a skillet for 2-3 minutes until onion is soft and transparent, then transfer contents of skillet to a bowl.*
2-2 1/2 cups/500-625 mL day-old white breadcubes — 1/2 inch/ 1 cm cubes	*Add breadcubes to bowl and mix together.*
1 large egg 1/2 cup/125 mL sour cream 1 tsp./5 mL lemon zest	*Add egg, sour cream and lemon zest to bowl and mix together.*
1/2 cup/125 mL fresh shrimp — or 1/2 cup/125 mL fresh crabmeat	*Add shrimp or crabmeat to bowl and gently mix together.*
salt *(to taste)* white pepper *(to taste)* 2 tbsp./30 mL finely chopped fresh dill	*Season with salt, pepper and dill.*
	Pre-heat oven to 350°F/180°C.
salt *(to taste)* white pepper *(to taste)* 1/8 tsp./pinch of paprika	*Season salmon, inside and out, with salt, pepper and paprika.*
2 tbsp./30 mL melted butter	*Drizzle with butter.*
	Stuff cavity of each fish with breadcube stuffing and put salmon on a buttered baking tray.
	Put baking tray in oven and bake for 20 minutes, basting occasionally with pan juices, until fish is done.
4 sprigs of fresh dill lemon-dill butter *(see below)*	*When fish is done, remove baking tray from oven and put salmon on a platter or individual plates. Garnish platter or plates with sprigs of dill and serve immediately. Serve with lemon-dill butter in a sauceboat on the side.*

(cont'd over)

Lemon-Dill Butter:

1 tbsp./15 mL peeled and finely chopped shallots
2 tbsp./30 mL dry white wine
juice of 1 lemon

Sauté shallots in white wine and lemon juice in a saucepan for approximately 1 minute.

4-5 tbsp./60-75 mL butter

Add butter to saucepan and blend in.

salt *(to taste)*
white pepper *(to taste)*
2 tbsp./30 mL finely chopped fresh dill

Season with salt, pepper and dill.

Transfer contents of saucepan to a sauceboat and serve warm.

Photo #7 *(page 167):* Saltwater Fish. *Foreground:* Baked Stuffed Baby Salmon; *background:* Baked Whole Red Snapper. Casserole and bowl *(foreground)* courtesy of Georg Jensen; platter *(background)* courtesy of W.H. Puddifoot.

CUBED SCALLOP OF MARINATED SALMON
BRAISED IN CHIANTI WITH FENNEL *Serves 4*
Fette di Salmone Brasato al Vino Rosa con Finocchio

1 1/2-2 lbs./700 g-1 kg fillet of fresh salmon, skin and bones removed — cut into 2 inch/5 cm scallops, then cut into 2 inch/5 cm cubes

Rinse cubes of salmon under cold running water and pat dry with paper towels.

1 1/2 cups/375 mL chianti — reserving 1 cup/250 mL chianti for braising

Put 1/2 cup/125 mL chianti in a baking dish.

Marinate salmon in chianti in baking dish in the refrigerator for 1 hour, then remove dish from refrigerator. Drain salmon and discard marinade.

salt *(to taste)*
freshly ground black pepper *(to taste)*
flour *(to coat)*

Season salmon with salt and pepper. Dredge in flour.

4 tbsp./60 mL olive oil

Sauté salmon in oil in a skillet for 2-3 minutes until lightly golden.

1/2 head of fennel, washed and sliced
1 whole clove of garlic, peeled

Add fennel and garlic to skillet and sauté for approximately 1 minute.

1 cup/250 mL chianti *(reserved above)*

Add chianti to skillet and bring to a boil. Reduce heat and simmer for approximately 3 minutes until wine has reduced to become the consistency of a glaze. Remove garlic from skillet.

2 tbsp./30 mL butter

Add butter to skillet and blend in. Coat salmon and fennel with glaze.

salt *(to taste)*
freshly ground black pepper *(to taste)*

Season with salt and pepper.

4 sprigs of fresh fennel

Transfer contents of skillet to a platter or individual plates. Garnish platter or plates with sprigs of fennel and serve immediately.

Photo #8 *(page 168)*: Saltwater Fish. *Clockwise from top:* Grilled Marinated Swordfish with Raspberry-Ginger Sauce; Pan-Fried Fillet of Ocean Perch with Eggplant and Olives; and Poached Rolled Fillet of Sole Stuffed with Smoked Salmon and Asparagus. Plate and platters courtesy of Georg Jensen.

GRILLED SALMON STEAK
WITH HERB BUTTER
Bistecca di Salmone alla Griglia con Burro Verde

Serves 4

4 (6-8 oz./175-250 g) fresh salmon steaks
salt *(to taste)*
freshly ground black pepper *(to taste)*
olive oil *(to coat)*

Rinse salmon steaks under cold running water and pat dry with paper towels. Season with salt and pepper. Brush with olive oil and put on a platter. Set aside.

1/4 tsp./1 mL finely chopped fresh parsley
1/4 tsp./1 mL finely chopped fresh basil
1/4 tsp./1 mL finely chopped fresh oregano
1/4 tsp./1 mL finely chopped fresh tarragon
1/4 tsp./1 mL fresh thyme
1/4 tsp./1 mL lemon pepper

Mix parsley, basil, oregano, tarragon, thyme and lemon pepper together in a bowl and sprinkle over salmon steaks on platter. Put platter in the refrigerator for 30 minutes, then remove platter from refrigerator.

1 lemon, cut in half

Put salmon steaks on the oiled rack of a barbecue and cook over hot coals for approximately 6 minutes per side, squeezing with lemon juice and turning to trellis-mark, until fish is done.

When fish is done, remove from barbecue and put on a platter or individual plates. Serve immediately.

herb butter *(see below)*

Serve with 1 tbsp./15 mL herb butter on top of each salmon steak.

Herb Butter:

3 tbsp./45 mL butter
— at room temperature
juice of 1/2 lemon
zest of 1/2 lemon
1/2 tsp./2 mL finely chopped fresh parsley
1/2 tsp./2 mL chopped fresh chives
1/4 tsp./1 mL finely chopped fresh dill
1/4 tsp./1 mL finely chopped fresh tarragon
1/4 tsp./1 mL fresh thyme
salt *(to taste)*
freshly ground black pepper *(to taste)*

Put butter, lemon juice, lemon zest, parsley, chives, dill, tarragon, thyme, salt and pepper in a mixing bowl and whip for approximately 10 minutes until butter triples in volume. Make herb butter at least 3 hours in advance of cooking recipe above and store in refrigerator until ready to use.

Leftover herb butter may be frozen and used at some other time.

GRILLED SKEWERS OF SALMON
WITH CAPER BUTTER
Spiedino di Salmone

Serves 4

1 1/2-2 lbs./700 g-1 kg fillet of fresh salmon, skin and bones removed — cut into 2 inch/5 cm cubes
salt *(to taste)*
freshly ground black pepper *(to taste)*
juice of 1 lemon
1 tbsp./15 mL brandy
1 tbsp./15 mL finely chopped fresh parsley
1 tbsp./15 mL peeled and finely chopped shallots

Rinse cubes of salmon under cold running water and pat dry with paper towels. Season with salt and pepper and put in a baking dish. Sprinkle with lemon juice, brandy, parsley and shallots. Put baking dish in the refrigerator for 30 minutes, then remove dish from refrigerator.

8 wooden skewers, soaked in cold water

Thread salmon onto water-soaked wooden skewers.

olive oil *(to coat)*

Brush salmon with oil.

Put skewers on the oiled rack of a barbecue and cook over hot coals, turning frequently, for 8-12 minutes until fish is just done.

caper butter *(see below)*

When fish is just done, remove skewers from barbecue and put on a platter or individual plates. Serve immediately. Serve with caper butter in a sauceboat on the side.

Caper Butter:

1 tbsp./15 mL peeled and finely chopped shallots
2 tbsp./30 mL dry white wine
juice of 1/2 lemon

Sauté shallots in white wine and lemon juice in a saucepan for approximately 1 minute.

4 tbsp./60 mL butter

Add butter to saucepan and blend in.

1 1/2 tbsp./20 mL drained capers

Add capers to saucepan and heat to warm.

Transfer contents of saucepan to a sauceboat and serve warm.

SALMON IN PAPILLOTE
Salmone al Cartoccio

Serves 4

4 (6-8 oz./175-250 g) fillets of fresh salmon

Rinse fillets of salmon under cold running water and pat dry with paper towels. Using a sharp knife, make a pocket-size incision in the side of each fillet and set aside.

4 tbsp./60 mL cream cheese
1 1/2 tbsp./20 mL Dijon mustard
1/2 tsp./2 mL freshly squeezed lemon juice
1/4 tsp./1 mL lemon zest
1 1/2 tbsp./20 mL finely chopped fresh dill
salt *(to taste)*
white pepper *(to taste)*

Mix cream cheese, mustard, lemon juice, lemon zest, dill, salt and pepper together in a bowl and stuff incision in fillets with cream cheese mixture.

salt *(to taste)*
white pepper *(to taste)*
juice of 1/2 lemon
2 tsp./10 mL butter
4 sprigs of fresh dill

Season salmon with salt and pepper. Sprinkle with lemon juice. Dab each fillet with 1/2 tsp./2 mL butter and put 1 sprig of dill on top of each fillet.

buttered parchment paper or aluminum foil

Put each fillet on a piece of buttered parchment paper or aluminum foil large enough to wrap the fillet.

Pre-heat oven to 400°F/200°C.

Seal parchment paper or aluminum foil and put sealed fillets on a baking tray.

Put baking tray in oven and cook for approximately 15 minutes.

1 lemon, cut into 4 wedges

Remove baking tray from oven and serve fillets of salmon in paper or foil on individual plates. Garnish plates with lemon wedges and serve immediately. Unwrap fillets at the table.

SAUTEED SALMON STEAKS
WITH BLACK BEAN SAUCE
Bistecca di Salmone all' Orientale

Serves 4

4 (6-8 oz./175-250 g) fresh salmon steaks
salt *(to taste)*
white pepper *(to taste)*
1/4 tsp./1 mL peeled and finely chopped garlic
1/2 tsp./2 mL peeled and finely chopped fresh ginger root
flour *(to dust)*

Rinse salmon steaks under cold running water and pat dry with paper towels. Season with salt and pepper. Sprinkle with garlic and ginger. Dust with flour.

1/4 cup/50 mL peanut oil

Sauté salmon in oil in a skillet for approximately 7 minutes per side, then remove from skillet, put on a platter, set aside and keep warm. Drain oil from skillet.

1 tbsp./15 mL peanut oil

Replenish oil in skillet.

1 large clove garlic, peeled and thinly sliced

Sauté garlic in oil in skillet until garlic begins to turn brown.

2 tbsp./30 mL black beans
2 tbsp./30 mL soy sauce
1 tbsp./15 mL brown sugar
1 tbsp./15 mL hot sesame oil
1 tbsp./15 mL white vinegar
2 tbsp./30 mL chicken stock *(see p. 7)*
1/8 tsp./pinch of seeded and finely chopped hot red chili pepper

Add black beans, soy sauce, brown sugar, sesame oil, vinegar, chicken stock and chili pepper to skillet, mix together and simmer for approximately 1 minute until mixture is warm.

Spoon contents of skillet over salmon steaks on platter and serve immediately. Serve directly from platter to individual plates.

SAUTEED SCALLOP OF SALMON
WITH ASTI SPUMANTE SAUCE
Salmone Classico

Serves 4

8 (3 1/2 oz./100 g) scallops of fresh salmon, skin and bones removed
salt *(to taste)*
white pepper *(to taste)*

Rinse scallops of salmon under cold running water and pat dry with paper towels. Gently pound scallops between 2 sheets of waxed paper until they are 1/4 inch/6 mm thick. Season with salt and pepper.

3 tbsp./45 mL butter

Sauté salmon in butter in a skillet for approximately 1 minute per side.

1/2 cup/125 mL asti spumante

Add asti spumante to skillet and simmer for approximately 1 minute, then remove scallops from skillet, put on a platter, set aside and keep warm. Reserve asti spumante in skillet and reduce by simmering for approximately 1 minute.

1/2 cup/125 mL whipping cream

Add cream to skillet, blend in and simmer for 2-3 minutes.

2 tbsp./30 mL butter

Add butter to skillet and blend in.

1 tsp./5 mL freshly squeezed lemon juice

Add lemon juice to skillet and blend in.

salt *(to taste)*
white pepper *(to taste)*

Season with salt and pepper.

1 tbsp./15 mL chopped fresh chives

Spoon contents of skillet over scallops of salmon on platter. Sprinkle with chives and serve immediately. Serve directly from platter to individual plates.

SARDINES
Sardine

Background: *Sardines are caught by fisherman in all the countries around the north Atlantic ocean and in the Mediterranean sea. They are eaten fresh in Europe, but, because they are highly perishable, they are canned, packed in oil, and are best-known in this form in North America. Sardines which are caught and canned on the East Coast of North America are actually a species of small herring. Herring, which are readily available in North America, can often be prepared the same way as sardines. Sardines are favourites as hors d' oeuvres.*

GRILLED SARDINES WITH OLIVE OIL, LEMON JUICE AND FENNEL
Sardine ai Ferri con Finocchio

Serves 4

2 lbs./1 kg whole fresh sardines, cleaned — 32-40 sardines
salt *(to taste)*
freshly ground black pepper *(to taste)*
juice of 1 lemon
1/2 medium fennel, washed and thinly sliced
1/4 cup/50 mL extra virgin olive oil

1/4 cup/50 mL extra virgin olive oil
juice of 1-2 lemons

Rinse sardines under cold running water and pat dry with paper towels. Season with salt and pepper and put in a baking dish. Sprinkle with lemon juice and fennel. Drizzle with olive oil. Put baking dish in the refrigerator for 1 hour, then remove dish from refrigerator.

Put sardines in an oiled grilling rack. Put grilling rack on the barbecue and cook sardines over hot coals for approximately 5 minutes until golden. Brush with olive oil and lemon juice while barbecuing.

When sardines are done, remove grilling rack from barbecue and put sardines on a platter. Serve immediately. Serve directly from platter to individual plates.

SEA BASS
Spigola

Background: *Many fish are passed off as sea bass. In the Mediterranean, the common sea bass is known as the sea wolf in both France and Italy. On the Atlantic side of France, the striped sea bass is found, which is a different fish. Other fish that are called sea bass are: ocean perch, grouper, Atlantic and Pacific rockfish, American sea bass or blackfish, Pacific ocean white sea bass, sand bass and black sea bass, the latter of which shows up in Chinese cuisine. On the Pacific coast, white sea bass is the species traditionally sold as sea bass. However, grouper is often available and can be cooked as if it were sea bass. In eastern North America, the fish that is bought as sea bass is likely to be American sea bass or French striped sea bass. Sea bass have firm-textured white flesh and excellent flavour. They are not to be confused with lake bass, which is a freshwater fish.*

BAKED AND GRATINEED
FILLET OF SEA BASS
Filetti di Spigola Gratinati

Serves 4

4 (8 oz./250 g) fillets of fresh sea bass
salt *(to taste)*
freshly ground black pepper *(to taste)*
dash of onion salt
dash of celery salt
juice of 1 lime
4 drops of Worcestershire sauce
4 drops of Tabasco sauce
1/2 tsp./2 mL finely chopped fresh marjoram
2 tbsp./30 mL extra virgin olive oil

Rinse fillets of sea bass under cold running water and pat dry with paper towels. Season with salt, pepper, onion salt and celery salt and put on a buttered baking tray. Sprinkle with lime juice, Worcestershire sauce, Tabasco sauce and marjoram. Drizzle with olive oil and set aside.

Pre-heat oven to 450°F/230°C.

6 tbsp./90 mL fresh fine white breadcrumbs
2 tbsp./30 mL freshly grated Parmesan cheese

Mix breadcrumbs and Parmesan cheese together in a bowl.

Sprinkle sea bass with breadcrumb mixture.

4 tsp./20 mL melted butter

Drizzle each fillet with 1 tsp./5 mL butter.

Put baking tray in oven and bake for approximately 12 minutes until golden brown.

4 sprigs of fresh marjoram
1 lime, cut into 4 wedges

Remove tray from oven and put fillets of sea bass on a platter or individual plates. Garnish each fillet of sea bass with 1 sprig of marjoram. Garnish platter or plates with lime wedges and serve immediately.

POACHED FILLET OF SEA BASS WITH OLIVE OIL, LEMON JUICE AND CILANTRO   *Serves 4*
Filetti di Spigola Olio e Limone

4 (6-8 oz./175-250 g) fillets of fresh
sea bass
salt *(to taste)*
freshly ground black pepper *(to taste)*
juice of 1 lemon
1/4 tsp./1 mL peeled and
finely chopped garlic
1/4 tsp./1 mL peeled and
finely chopped fresh ginger root
2 tbsp./30 mL finely chopped
fresh cilantro
2 tbsp./30 mL extra virgin olive oil

Rinse fillets of sea bass under cold running water and pat dry with paper towels. Season with salt and pepper and put in a buttered baking pan. Sprinkle with lemon juice, garlic, ginger and cilantro. Drizzle with olive oil and put baking pan in the refrigerator for 30 minutes, then remove pan from refrigerator.

Pre-heat oven to 375°F/190°C.

juice of 1 lemon
4 tsp./20 mL extra virgin olive oil
12 sprigs of fresh cilantro
4 slices of lemon

Sprinkle sea bass with lemon juice and drizzle each fillet with 1 tsp./5 mL olive oil. Put 3 sprigs of cilantro and 1 slice of lemon on top of each fillet.

1/2 cup/125 mL chicken stock
(see p. 7)

Add chicken stock to baking pan and bring to a boil on top of the stove.

buttered paper

Cover baking pan with a sheet of buttered paper. Put pan in oven and poach for 8-12 minutes, then remove pan from oven and put fillets, with sprigs of cilantro and lemon slices on top, on a platter or individual plates.

4 tsp./20 mL extra virgin olive oil
4 sprigs of fresh cilantro
1 lemon, cut into 4 wedges

Drizzle each fillet of sea bass with 1 tsp./5 mL olive oil and put 1 fresh sprig of cilantro on top of each fillet. Garnish platter or plates with lemon wedges and serve immediately.

SKATE
Razza

Background: *Skate, or ray, are sold in wings which range in weight from 1-5 lbs./500 g-2.5 kg. Skate is highly perishable and should be eaten fresh. Elsewise, it can pick up an ammonia odour. Skate is found in the Mediterranean sea and in the north Pacific and north Atlantic ocean. They are flat, scaleless fish with unusually broad wings and long, thick tails. They are olive above and tan below and are caught all year round, but are most available from May to July. They are medium in fat content.*

POACHED SKATE SERVED
WITH OIL AND VINEGAR CONDIMENTS *Serves 4*
Razza alla Maniera Italiana

2 lbs./1 kg wings of fresh skate, bones removed — cut into 4 (8 oz./250 g) portions
salt *(to taste)*
freshly ground black pepper *(to taste)*

Rinse skate under cold running water and pat dry with paper towels. Season with salt and pepper and set aside.

8 cups/2 L cold water
1/2 small onion, peeled and chopped
1/2 small carrot, peeled and sliced
1/2 stalk of celery, washed and sliced
1/2 medium leek, washed and chopped — use only the white part
juice of 1 lemon
3 tbsp./45 mL white vinegar
1 tbsp./15 mL salt
1/2 tsp./2 mL crushed white peppercorns
1 bay leaf
2 sprigs of fresh parsley, chopped
1 sprig of fresh thyme

Make a court bouillon by putting water, onion, carrot, celery, leek, lemon juice, vinegar, salt, peppercorns, bay leaf, parsley and thyme in a pot and bringing to a boil. Reduce heat to a simmer.

Drop skate into pot and poach for 12-15 minutes.

extra virgin olive oil *(to accompany)*
balsamic vinegar *(to accompany)*

Remove skate from pot and dab with a cloth or paper towel to dry. Put skate on a platter and serve immediately. Serve directly from platter to individual plates. Serve with oil and vinegar condiments on the side.

SAUTEED SKATE IN BLACK BUTTER *Serves 4*
Razza al Burro Nero

2 lbs./1 kg wings of fresh skate, bones removed — cut into 4 (8 oz./250 g) portions
salt *(to taste)*
white pepper *(to taste)*
juice of 1/2 lemon
2 drops of Worcestershire sauce
flour *(to coat)*

Rinse skate under cold running water and pat dry with paper towels. Season with salt and pepper. Sprinkle with lemon juice and Worcestershire sauce. Dredge in flour.

3 tbsp./45 mL vegetable oil
1 tbsp./15 mL butter

Sauté skate in oil and butter in a skillet for 6-7 minutes per side, then drain oil from skillet. Leave skate in skillet and set aside.

3 tbsp./45 mL butter

Melt butter in another skillet. Allow butter to foam and turn light brown.

Pour butter over skate in skillet and heat. Butter will turn brown and give fish a nutty taste.

1 tbsp./15 mL finely chopped fresh parsley
1 lemon, cut into 4 wedges

Transfer contents of skillet to a platter or individual plates. Sprinkle with parsley. Garnish platter or plates with lemon wedges and serve immediately.

SMELT
Sperlano

Background: *Smelt are small trout-like species which seldom run upriver beyond the tide line. They are transparent olive to bottle green on their backs, with paler sides and silver underbellies. They average 6-10 inches/12-20 cm in length and are found in the North Sea, the Baltic, the English Channel, the Atlantic, and at the mouths of rivers and in the Great Lakes in North America. Smelt are available all year round, but are best taken in the spring and fall. Freshly caught, they have a strong smell, but they are delicate in flavour and have sweet-tasting flesh like watermelon. They are best served pan-fried and, as such, are regarded as one of the finest of all fish dishes.*

BAKED SMELTS
WITH ONIONS AND CIDER VINEGAR   Serves 4
Sperlani al Forno con Cipolle e Aceto

2 lbs./1 kg whole fresh smelts, cleaned, with the heads off — 32-48 smelts
salt *(to taste)*
freshly ground black pepper *(to taste)*

Rinse smelts under cold running water and pat dry with paper towels. Season with salt and pepper. Put smelts on an oiled baking tray and set aside.

Pre-heat oven to 400°F/200°C.

2 medium onions, peeled and julienned
1/4 cup/50 mL olive oil

Sauté onions in oil in a skillet for 3-4 minutes until they begin to turn brown.

4 tbsp./60 mL cider vinegar
3 tbsp./45 mL finely chopped fresh parsley

Add vinegar and parsley to skillet and stir to coat onions.

salt *(to taste)*
freshly ground black pepper *(to taste)*

Season with salt and pepper.

Spoon contents of skillet over smelts on baking tray. Put baking tray in oven and bake for approximately 5 minutes until just done.

2 tbsp./30 mL finely chopped fresh parsley

Remove baking tray from oven and put smelts and onions on a platter. Spoon pan liquid over top of platter and sprinkle with parsley. Serve immediately. Serve directly from platter to individual plates.

PAN-FRIED SMELTS
WITH CAPER MAYONNAISE
Sperlani con Maionese

Serves 4

2 lbs./1 kg whole fresh smelts, cleaned, with the heads off — 32-48 smelts
salt (*to taste*)
freshly ground black pepper (*to taste*)
juice of 1 lemon
flour (*to coat*)

Rinse smelts under cold running water and pat dry with paper towels. Season with salt and pepper. Sprinkle with lemon juice. Dredge in flour.

1/2 cup/125 mL clarified butter

Fry smelts, several at a time, in butter in a skillet for 2-3 minutes, then remove from skillet and drain on paper towels.

2 lemons, cut into 8 wedges
1 1/2 cups/375 mL caper mayonnaise (*see below*)

Put smelts on a platter. Garnish platter with lemon wedges and serve immediately. Serve directly from platter to individual plates. Serve with caper mayonnaise in a bowl on the side.

Caper Mayonnaise:

1 cup/250 mL mayonnaise (*see p. 14*)

Put mayonnaise in a bowl.

2 tbsp./30 mL drained and chopped capers
juice of 1/2 lemon
1 tsp./5 mL finely chopped fresh parsley

Add capers, lemon juice and parsley to bowl and mix together.

salt (*to taste*)
white pepper (*to taste*)

Season with salt and pepper.

SOLE
Sogliola

Background: *Sole are known worldwide. They are best-known to Europeans as Dover sole. Pacific and Atlantic sole are members of the flounder family and are named locally. On the Pacific coast, there is English sole, also known as lemon sole, common sole or California sole, which is different from the accepted lemon sole of Europe; rock sole; petrale sole; and rex sole. On the Atlantic coast, there is lemon sole, which are winter flounder; and gray or white sole, which are witch flounder (see flounder). Sole live on the bottom of the ocean, all but invisible to their enemies and prey, and they like cold water. The colour of their skin varies according to the colour of the bottom of the ocean. The whiter the underside, the better the texture and flavour of the fish. Sole are low in fat content and have fine-grained white flesh which has a delicate flavour. They are the most popular flatfish and the best-flavoured and most digestible of all fish.*

PAN-FRIED FILLET OF SOLE
WITH HOMEMADE TARTAR SAUCE
Serves 4
Sogliola Dorati Salsa Tartara

4 (6-8 oz./175-250 g) fillets of fresh sole
salt *(to taste)*
white pepper *(to taste)*
juice of 1/2 lemon
dash of Worcestershire sauce
flour *(to dust)*

Rinse fillets of sole under cold running water and pat dry with paper towels. Season with salt and pepper. Sprinkle with lemon juice and Worcestershire sauce. Dust with flour.

4 tbsp./60 mL vegetable oil
2 tbsp./30 mL butter

Fry sole in oil and butter in a skillet for 3-4 minutes per side until golden brown, then remove from skillet and drain on paper towels. Put sole on a platter, set aside and keep warm.

1 tbsp./15 mL finely chopped fresh parsley
1 lemon, cut into 4 wedges
2 cups/500 mL tartar sauce
(see p. 10)

Sprinkle sole with parsley and garnish platter with lemon wedges. Serve immediately. Serve directly from platter to individual plates. Serve with tartar sauce in a bowl on the side.

PAN-FRIED FILLET OF SOLE
WITH LEMON BUTTER
Sogliola alla Mugnaia

Serves 4

4 (6-8 oz./175-250 g) fillets of fresh sole
salt *(to taste)*
white pepper *(to taste)*
juice of 1/2 lemon
dash of Worcestershire sauce
flour *(to dust)*

Rinse fillets of sole under cold running water and pat dry with paper towels. Season with salt and pepper. Sprinkle with lemon juice and Worcestershire sauce. Dust with flour.

4 tbsp./60 mL vegetable oil
4 tbsp./60 mL butter

Fry sole in oil and butter in a skillet for 3-4 minutes per side until golden brown, then remove from skillet and drain on paper towels. Put sole on a platter, set aside and keep warm.

4 tbsp./60 mL lemon butter
(see p. 95)
1 tbsp./15 mL finely chopped fresh parsley
1 lemon, cut into 4 wedges

Drizzle each fillet of sole with 1 tbsp./15 mL lemon butter and sprinkle parsley over all 4 fillets. Garnish platter with lemon wedges and serve immediately. Serve directly from platter to individual plates.

PAN-FRIED FILLET OF SOLE
WITH PINE NUTS
Sogliola Fritte

Serves 4

4 (6-8 oz./175-250 g) fillets of fresh sole
salt *(to taste)*
white pepper *(to taste)*
juice of 1/2 lemon
dash of Worcestershire sauce
flour *(to dust)*

Rinse fillets of sole under cold running water and pat dry with paper towels. Season with salt and pepper. Sprinkle with lemon juice and Worcestershire sauce. Dust with flour.

2 tbsp./30 mL olive oil
2 tbsp./30 mL butter

Fry sole in oil and butter in a skillet for aproximately 3 minutes per side until lightly golden, then remove from skillet, put on a platter, set aside and keep warm.

3 firm, ripe tomatoes, eyes removed and scored "x" on top

Blanch tomatoes in a pot of rapidly boiling water for 20 seconds, then plunge into a pot of cold water to stop the cooking. Peel, seed and chop tomatoes.

Add tomatoes to skillet and simmer for 3-4 minutes.

2 tbsp./30 mL toasted pine nuts
2 tbsp./30 mL pitted and sliced black Calamata olives
1 tbsp./15 mL drained capers
1 tsp./5 mL finely chopped fresh tarragon

Add pine nuts, olives, capers and tarragon to skillet and simmer for 1-2 minutes.

1 tbsp./15 mL extra virgin olive oil

Add olive oil to skillet and blend in.

salt *(to taste)*
white pepper *(to taste)*

Season with salt and pepper.

Spoon contents of skillet over fillets of sole on platter and serve immediately. Serve directly from platter to individual plates.

POACHED FILLET OF SOLE
WITH ORANGE SAUCE
Filetto di Sogliola all' Arancia

Serves 4

4 (6-8 oz./175-250 g) fillets of
fresh sole
salt *(to taste)*
freshly ground black pepper *(to taste)*

Rinse fillets of sole under cold running water and pat dry with paper towels. Season with salt and pepper and put in a buttered baking dish.

Pre-heat oven to 350°F/180°C.

juice of 2 oranges
freshly ground black pepper *(to taste)*

Pour orange juice over sole and sprinkle with pepper.

1/2 cup/125 mL dry white wine

Add white wine to baking dish.

buttered paper

Cover baking dish with a sheet of buttered paper. Put dish in oven and poach for 8-10 minutes, then remove dish from oven, put fillets on a platter, set aside and keep warm. Reserve liquid in dish and transfer to a saucepan.

2 tbsp./30 mL whipping cream

Add cream to saucepan, blend in and simmer for approximately 1 minute, then remove saucepan from heat.

4 tbsp./60 mL butter

Add butter to saucepan and blend in.

salt *(to taste)*
freshly ground black pepper *(to taste)*

Season with salt and pepper.

8 sections of orange,
peeled and seeded
zest of 1/2 orange, blanched

Spoon contents of saucepan over fillets of sole on platter. Garnish each fillet of sole with 2 sections of orange and sprinkle orange zest over all. Serve immediately. Serve directly from platter to individual plates.

POACHED ROLLED FILLET OF SOLE
STUFFED WITH SMOKED SALMON
AND ASPARAGUS
Serves 4
Involtini di Sogliola con Salmone Affumicato e Asparagi

8 (4 oz./125 g) small fillets of fresh sole salt *(to taste)* white pepper *(to taste)* juice of 1/2 lemon	*Rinse fillets of sole under cold running water and pat dry with paper towels. Gently pound fillets between 2 sheets of plastic wrap until they are 1/4 inch/ 6 mm thick. Season with salt and pepper. Spinkle with lemon juice. Lay fillets on a flat work surface.*
1/4 lb./125 g sliced fresh smoked salmon — 8 thin slices approximately the same shape as each fillet of sole	*Lay 1 slice of smoked salmon on top of each fillet of sole and set aside.*
16-24 small spears of fresh asparagus, washed, peeled and trimmed to fit width of sole	*Blanch asparagus in a pot of rapidly boiling water for approximately 2 minutes, then freshen in a pot of cold water. Lay 2-3 asparagus spears crosswise on top of each slice of smoked salmon.*
	Roll fillets of sole, stuffed with smoked salmon and asparagus, and put, seam side down, in a buttered baking pan.
	Pre-heat oven to 350°F/180°C.
1 cup/250 mL dry white wine	*Add white wine to baking pan and bring to a boil on top of the stove.*
buttered paper	*Cover baking pan with a sheet of buttered paper. Put pan in oven and poach for 15 minutes until fish is done. Remove pan from oven, put stuffed fillets on a platter, set aside and keep warm. Reserve liquid in pan and transfer to a saucepan. Reduce liquid in saucepan by one-half.*
1 cup/250 mL whipping cream	*Add cream to saucepan, blend in and simmer for 3-5 minutes until sauce thickens slightly, then remove saucepan from heat.*
2 tbsp./30 mL butter	*Add butter to saucepan and blend in.*
juice of 1/2 lemon	*Add lemon juice to saucepan and blend in.*

salt *(to taste)*	Season with salt and pepper.
white pepper *(to taste)*	

Spoon contents of saucepan over stuffed fillets of sole on platter and serve immediately. Serve directly from platter to individual plates.

SAUTEED FILLET OF SOLE WITH MUSHROOMS AND CAPERS
Filetto di Sogliola con Funghi e Capperi

Serves 4

4 (6-8 oz./175-250 g) fillets of fresh sole salt *(to taste)* white pepper *(to taste)* flour *(to dust)*	Rinse fillets of sole under cold running water and pat dry with paper towels. Season with salt and pepper. Dust with flour.
2 tbsp./30 mL olive oil 2 tbsp./30 mL butter	Sauté sole in oil and butter in a skillet for approximately 3 minutes per side until lightly golden, then remove from skillet, put on a platter, set aside and keep warm. Drain oil from skillet.
1 1/2 cups/375 mL cleaned and thinly sliced fresh mushrooms 3 tbsp./45 mL dry white wine juice of 1 lemon	Sauté mushrooms in white wine and lemon juice in skillet for 2-3 minutes.
2 tbsp./30 mL drained capers	Add capers to skillet and heat to warm, remove skillet from heat.
3 tbsp./45 mL butter	Add butter to skillet and blend in.
salt *(to taste)* white pepper *(to taste)*	Season with salt and pepper.

Spoon contents of skillet over fillets of sole on platter and serve immediately. Serve directly from platter to individual plates.

STURGEON
Storione

Background: *Sturgeon are pale grey saltwater fish. They have plates along their backs and sides. Because they are often found at the mouths of rivers, they have a freshwater taste. They range in weight from 10 lbs./5 kg and are caught in the winter and spring. They are sold, fresh and frozen, in large fillets, or blocks, fillets and steaks and are widely available in the North American market. Sturgeon are high in fat content and their dense, firm flesh, which is almost meat-like, has a mild, sweet flavour.*

PAN-FRIED FILLET OF STURGEON WITH WILD MUSHROOMS
Filetti di Storione con Funghi di Bosco
Serves 4

4 (6-8 oz./175-250 g) fillets of fresh sturgeon
salt *(to taste)*
freshly ground black pepper *(to taste)*
juice of 1 lemon
1/4 tsp./1 mL peeled and finely chopped garlic
1/4 tsp./1 mL finely chopped fresh marjoram
1/4 tsp./1 mL finely chopped fresh oregano
flour *(to dust)*

Rinse fillets of sturgeon under cold running water and pat dry with paper towels. Season with salt and pepper and put in a baking dish. Sprinkle with lemon juice, garlic, marjoram and oregano. Put baking dish in refrigerator for 20 minutes, then remove dish from refrigerator and dust fillets with flour.

2 tbsp./30 mL olive oil
2 tbsp./30 mL butter

Fry sturgeon in oil and butter in a skillet for 6-8 minutes on 1 side, then turn fillets over.

1/2 lb./250 g fresh Chanterelle or Porcini mushrooms, cleaned and sliced
1 tbsp./15 mL peeled and finely chopped shallots

Add mushrooms and shallots to skillet and fry sturgeon on other side for 1-2 minutes.

1 1/2 cups/375 mL tomato sauce *(see p. 11)*

Add tomato sauce to skillet and simmer for 5-6 minutes until fish is done.

2 tbsp./30 mL extra virgin olive oil

Drizzle with olive oil.

salt *(to taste)*
freshly ground black pepper *(to taste)*

Season with salt and pepper.

4 small sprigs of fresh oregano

Transfer contents of skillet to a platter or individual plates. Garnish each fillet of sturgeon with 1 sprig of oregano and serve immediately.

POACHED FILLET OF STURGEON
WITH ASPARAGUS IN CREAM SAUCE   *Serves 4*
Filetti di Storione con Asparagi

4 (6-8 oz./175-250 g) fillets of fresh sturgeon salt *(to taste)* white pepper *(to taste)* juice of 1 lemon 4 sprigs of fresh parsley 4 sprigs of fresh thyme	*Rinse fillets of sturgeon under cold running water and pat dry with paper towels. Season with salt and pepper and put in a buttered baking pan. Sprinkle with lemon juice and put 1 sprig of parsley and 1 sprig of thyme on top of each fillet.*
	Pre-heat oven to 350°F/180°C.
1/2 cup/125 mL dry white wine	*Add white wine to baking pan and bring to a boil on top of the stove.*
buttered paper	*Cover baking pan with a sheet of buttered paper. Put pan in oven and poach for 6-8 minutes, then remove pan from oven and uncover.*
12 small spears of fresh asparagus, washed, peeled and sliced on an angle	*Lay 3 asparagus spears on top of each fillet of sturgeon.*
1 cup/250 mL whipping cream	*Add cream to baking pan.*
	Re-cover baking pan and return to oven. Poach for an additional 3-4 minutes, then remove pan from oven and uncover. Put fillets, with asparagus on top, on a platter. Set platter aside and keep warm. Reserve liquid in pan and transfer to a saucepan.
2 tbsp./30 mL butter	*Add butter to saucepan and blend in.*
juice of 1 lemon	*Add lemon juice to saucepan and blend in.*
salt *(to taste)* white pepper *(to taste)*	*Season with salt and pepper.*
1 lemon, cut into 4 wedges	*Spoon contents of saucepan over fillets of sturgeon, with asparagus on top, on platter. Garnish platter with lemon wedges and serve immediately. Serve directly from platter to individual plates.*

SWORDFISH
Pesce Spada

Background: *Swordfish live in tropical and temperate waters and have long been popular in the Mediterranean. They are dark grey on top and yellowish underneath. They have an average weight of 150 lbs./75 kg and are moderate in fat content. They are available fresh all year round, but are more available in the summer and early fall. Swordfish come in large fillets, or blocks, and in steaks. They are the most meat-like in texture of all fish and are a favourite fish for grilling.*

GRILLED MARINATED SWORDFISH
WITH RASPBERRY-GINGER SAUCE
Pesce Spada ai Lamponi

Serves 4

4 (8 oz./250 g) fillets of fresh swordfish	*Rinse fillets of swordfish under cold running water and pat dry with paper towels.*
marinade *(see next page)*	*Put swordfish in marinade in a baking dish in the refrigerator for 2-3 hours, then remove dish from refrigerator. Drain swordfish and reserve marinade for basting while swordfish is barbecuing.*
1 lemon, cut in half	*Put swordfish on the oiled rack of a barbecue and cook over hot coals for 5-7 minutes per side, basting with marinade and squeezing with lemon juice, until fish is done. Do not overcook.*
raspberry-ginger sauce *(see next page)* 8-12 slices of drained pickled ginger — gari 4 tips of fresh chives 4 whole raspberries	*When fish is done, remove from barbecue and put on a platter. Spoon raspberry-ginger sauce over fillets of swordfish on platter and garnish each fillet with 2-3 slices of pickled ginger, 1 chive tip and 1 whole raspberry. Serve immediately. Serve directly from platter to individual plates.*

Marinade:

1/2 cup/125 mL olive oil
juice of 1 lemon
2 cloves of garlic, peeled
and crushed
1 tbsp./15 mL peeled and
finely chopped fresh ginger root
1 tsp./5 mL finely chopped
fresh parsley
1 tsp./5 mL finely chopped
fresh oregano
salt *(to taste)*
freshly ground black pepper *(to taste)*

Mix olive oil, lemon juice, garlic, ginger, parsley, oregano, salt and pepper together in a baking dish.

Raspberry-Ginger Sauce:

1 1/2 tbsp./20 mL peeled and finely
chopped fresh ginger root
1 tsp./5 mL peeled and
finely chopped garlic
1/2 cup/125 mL dry sherry
1 tbsp./15 mL white wine vinegar

Simmer ginger and garlic in sherry and vinegar in a saucepan until liquid has reduced by one-half.

1 1/2 cups/375 mL whole fresh
raspberries — or 1 (10 oz./300 g) pkg.
of frozen unsweetened raspberries,
thawed

Add raspberries to saucepan, stir in and simmer for 3-5 minutes, then strain contents of saucepan by pressing through a sieve into another saucepan. Discard seeds in sieve. Bring sauce in saucepan to a boil, then reduce heat.

1 tbsp./15 mL butter

Add butter to saucepan, blend in and simmer for 1-2 minutes.

salt *(to taste)*
freshly ground black pepper *(to taste)*

Season with salt and pepper.

PAN-FRIED SWORDFISH
WITH STONEGROUND MUSTARD SAUCE *Serves 4*
Pesce Spada in Padella alla Senape

4 (8 oz./250 g) fillets of fresh swordfish
salt *(to taste)*
freshly ground black pepper *(to taste)*
juice of 1 lemon
3 tbsp./45 mL stoneground mustard
flour *(to dust)*

Rinse fillets of swordfish under cold running water and pat dry with paper towels. Season with salt and pepper. Sprinkle with lemon juice. Rub with mustard and dust with flour.

1/4 cup/50 mL peanut oil

Fry swordfish in oil in a skillet for 6-7 minutes per side until fish is just done. Do not overcook. Remove fillets from skillet, put on a platter, set aside and keep warm. Drain oil from skillet.

1/4 cup/50 mL dry white wine
1/4 cup/50 mL chicken stock
(see p. 7)

Add white wine and chicken stock to skillet and mix together. Bring contents of skillet to a boil, then reduce heat.

2 tbsp./30 mL stoneground mustard

Add mustard to skillet, blend in and simmer for approximately 2 minutes.

2 tbsp./30 mL whipping cream
1 tbsp./15 mL butter

Add cream and butter to skillet, blend in and simmer for approximately 1 minute.

1 tbsp./15 mL finely chopped fresh parsley

Spoon contents of skillet over fillets of swordfish on platter. Sprinkle with parsley and serve immediately. Serve directly from platter to individual plates.

TUNA
Tonno

Background: *There are four major species of tuna: albacore, yellowfin, bluefin and bonito tuna. Albacore tuna are found only in tropical and temperate waters. They are steel grey or blue in colour and have an average weight of 40 lbs./20 kg. They are caught in the summer and early fall and are sold as fillets and steaks. Yellowfin and bluefin tuna are wider ranging and are much larger, with an average weight of 300 lbs./150 kg. Their flesh is darker in colour and more flavourful than albacore tuna and they are available all year round, but more available in the summer. Albacore tuna is marketed canned as ''white meat tuna'' and, as such, fetches the highest price, but, fresh, it is the least expensive tuna. Yellowfin tuna is marketed canned as ''light meat tuna'' and, fresh, it is in demand for sashimi and sushi. Bonito, or bonita, tuna are found in temperate waters and range in weight from 5 lbs./2.5 kg and up. They are available from late fall to early summer and are usually sold as fillets. They have a moderate flavour. Tuna are probably the strongest and fastest fish in the ocean. Canned, they are probably the best-known fish in the world, but they are gaining popularity as a fresh fish.*

GRILLED MARINATED FILLET OF TUNA   Serves 4
Tonno ai Ferri

4 (8 oz./250 g) fillets of fresh tuna	*Rinse fillets of tuna under cold running water and pat dry with paper towels.*
marinade *(see below)*	*Put tuna in marinade in a baking dish in the refrigerator for 1 hour, then remove dish from refrigerator. Drain tuna and reserve marinade for basting while tuna is barbecuing.*
1 lime, cut in half	*Put tuna on the oiled rack of a barbecue and cook over hot coals for 5-7 minutes per side, basting with marinade and squeezing with lime juice, until fish is done. Do not overcook — fish should be moist and still pink inside.*
4 tsp./20 mL extra virgin olive oil 2 limes, cut in half	*When fish is done, remove from barbecue and put on a platter or individual plates. Drizzle each fillet of tuna with 1 tsp./5 mL olive oil and serve with lime halves. Serve immediately.*

(cont'd over)

Marinade:

1/2 cup/125 mL olive oil
juice of 1 lime
1 tsp./5 mL peeled and
finely chopped garlic
1 tsp./5 mL finely chopped
fresh parsley
1 tsp./5 mL finely chopped
fresh oregano
freshly ground black pepper *(to taste)*

Mix olive oil, lime juice, garlic, parsley, oregano and pepper together in a baking dish.

SAUTEED CUBED FILLET OF TUNA MARINATED IN WHITE WINE AND SERVED ON A BED OF SPINACH
Serves 4
Tonno Tutto Verde

2 lbs./1 kg fillet of fresh tuna
— cut into 2 inch/5 cm cubes

Rinse cubes of tuna under cold running water and pat dry with paper towels.

1 cup/250 mL dry white wine
2 shallots, peeled and sliced

Put white wine and shallots in a baking dish.

Marinate tuna in white wine in baking dish in the refrigerator for 1-2 hours, then remove dish from refrigerator. Drain tuna and discard marinade.

freshly ground black pepper *(to taste)*
flour *(to dust)*

Season tuna with pepper and dust with flour.

1/4 cup/50 mL peanut oil

Sauté tuna in oil in a skillet for 6-8 minutes until golden brown, then remove from skillet and drain on paper towels. Set aside and keep warm.

5 bunches of fresh spinach,
washed and stemmed
1/4 cup/50 mL dry white wine
juice of 1/2 lemon
1/2 tsp./2 mL peeled and
finely chopped garlic
salt *(to taste)*
freshly ground black pepper *(to taste)*

Cook spinach in a pot containing white wine, lemon juice, garlic, salt and pepper for only 1 minute until spinach has just wilted, then drain pot and squeeze excess liquid from spinach.

juice of 1 lemon
4 tsp./20 mL extra virgin olive oil

Arrange spinach on a platter. Arrange tuna on top of spinach. Sprinkle with lemon juice and drizzle with olive oil. Serve immediately. Serve directly from platter to individual plates.

PAN-FRIED MARINATED FILLET OF TUNA *Serves 4*
Tonno Marinato Fatto in Padella

4 (8 oz./250 g) fillets of fresh tuna	*Rinse fillets of tuna under cold running water and pat dry with paper towels.*
marinade *(see below)*	*Put tuna in marinade in a baking dish in the refrigerator for 1 hour, then remove dish from refrigerator. Drain tuna and discard marinade.*
3 tbsp./45 mL olive oil	*Fry tuna in oil in a skillet for approximately 5 minutes per side until brown. Do not overcook. Remove tuna from skillet, put on a platter, set aside and keep warm.*
1 large firm, ripe tomato, eye removed and scored ''x'' on top	*Blanch tomato in a pot of rapidly boiling water for 20 seconds, then plunge into a pot of cold water to stop the cooking. Peel, seed and chop tomato.*
	Put tomato in a bowl.
2 scallions, washed and chopped 1/4 cup/50 mL extra virgin olive oil juice of 1 lemon 2 tbsp./30 mL finely chopped fresh basil salt *(to taste)* freshly ground black pepper *(to taste)*	*Add scallions, olive oil, lemon juice, basil, salt and pepper to bowl and gently mix together.*
	Spoon tomato mixture over fillets of tuna on platter and serve immediately. Serve directly from platter to individual plates.

Marinade:

1/4 cup/50 mL extra virgin olive oil juice of 1/2 lemon zest of 1/2 lemon 1 tsp./5 mL peeled and finely chopped garlic 2 tbsp./30 mL finely chopped flat-leaved Italian parsley freshly ground black pepper *(to taste)*	*Mix olive oil, lemon juice, lemon zest, garlic, parsley and pepper together in a baking dish.*

ACKNOWLEDGEMENTS

Thank you to the following for the loan of props for the photography: Gert and Birgit Petersen of Georg Jensen; Patrice Taylor of Basic Stock Cookware; Evelyn Springer; Linda Alexander of Tools & Techniques; and Kim and Olive Herendry of W.H. Puddifoot. Georg Jensen has stores in Toronto and Vancouver.

Research for this book was done under the guidance of the Department of Fisheries and Oceans, Government of Canada. Special thanks to Betty Fitzsimmons; and to Cynthia Babchuk for the initial research. Information on orange roughy was provided by the New Zealand consulate.

Umberto Menghi would like to thank Ron Lammie for his contribution to this book; and Marian Babchuk. Thanks also to Jahan Khazali, Gianni Picchi and Gertie Fuss; and to Kim Fahlman for the hair.

Ron Lammie would like to thank Louise Lammie and his children: Carissa, Nicholas and Kelsey — "More recipes, Daddy!" He would also like to thank Ian Milford for his assistance with the food for photography.

David Robinson would like to thank Zonda Nellis; and Alexandra Elisabeth Robinson for not messing up the manuscript. Thanks also to Dolma Tsering; and to Derik Murray, Marthe Love, Michael Morissette, Frank Vena, Brian Daisley, Scott Wanless, Jay Shaw and Wendy Darling at Derik Murray Photography Inc.

And thank you, Ron. And thank you, both Grandmas.